Indonesia Information

Tourist Guide, History, Bali Travel Environment

Author
David Mills.

SONITTEC PUBLISHING. All rights reserved. No part of this publication may be reproduced, distributed, or transmitted in any form or by any means, including photocopying, recording, or other electronic or mechanical methods, without the prior written permission of the publisher, except in the case of brief quotations embodied in critical reviews and certain other noncommercial uses permitted by copyright law. For permission requests, write to the publisher, addressed "Attention: Permissions Coordinator," at the address below.

Copyright © 2019 Sonittec Publishing
All Rights Reserved

First Printed: 2019.

Publisher:
SONITTEC LTD
College House, 2nd Floor
17 King Edwards Road,
Ruislip
London
HA4 7AE.

Table of Content

SUMMARY..1
INTRODUCTION..4
HISTORY...8
    EARLY HISTORY OF INDONESIAN CULTURE 8
    MATARAM (MEDANG) CULTURE.. 10
    PRAMBANAN AND BOROBODUR 14
    WAYANG STYLE OF THE EAST JAVANESE PERIOD 16
    MAJAPAHIT CULTURE.. 20
    IMPACT OF ISLAM ON INDONESIAN CULTURE................................. 24
    INDONESIAN CULTURE DURING THE COLONIAL PERIOD 28
    INDONESIAN CULTURE UNDER SUKARNO ANF SUHARTO................... 32
    CULTURE CHANGES IN POST-SUHARTO INDONESIA 36
CULTURE AND ARTS IN INDONESIA 41
    DIVERSITY OF INDONESIA'S CULTURE.. 45
    JAVA, INDONESIA'S CULTURAL HEART 46
    TRADITIONAL CULTURE OF INDONESIA 48
    SUPPORT FOR THE ARTS.. 51
    CULTURE WARS BETWEEN INDONESIA AND MALAYSIA 53
    CULTURAL WAR BETWEEN MALAYSIA AND INDONESIA 54
    CULTURAL WAR BETWEEN MALAYSIA AND INDONESIA GET UGLY 57
    BITTER FEELINGS BEHIND THE CULTURAL WAR BETWEEN MALAYSIA AND INDONESIA 59
INDONESIAN LITERATURE..64
    MAJAPAHIT LITERATURE AND THE NAGARAKERTAGAMA................... 68
    LITERATURE FROM THE DUTCH PERIOD IN INDONESIA...................... 70
    MODERN LITERATURE IN INDONESIA 71
    MODERN WRITERS AND BOOKS IN INDONESIA................................ 73
    LACK OF ENGLISH TRANSLATIONS AND INTEREST IN INDONESIAN LITERATURE 76
    EFFORT TO GET INDONESIAN LITERATURE TRANSLATED TO ENGLISH.... 79
    SAMAN, AYU UTAMI AND SEX 82
    SASTRA WANGI: INDONESIA'S SEXY FEMINIST LITERARY MOVEMENT... 85
    INDONESIA'S TWELVE-YEAR-OLD NOVELIST................................... 91

HISTORY AND CULTURE OF BALI 95
BALI TRAVEL GUIDE 107
  THINGS TO DO IN BALI 107
    Yeh Gangga Offroad - Bali 108
    Blanco Renaissance Museum - Bali 109
    Bali Orchid Garden - Bali 111
    The Chillhouse - Bali 113
    Eka Karya Botanic Garden - Bali 114
    S2S CrossFit - Bali 119
    Celebrity Fitness - Bali 120
    Ubud Fitness Center - Bali 121
    Sunrise School of Surfing - Bali 122
    Bali Zoo - Bali 123
    Bali Bird Park - Bali 125
    Amed Dive Centre - Bali 127
    Taman Nusa Cultural Park - Bali 128
    Dojo Aora Judo - Bali 129
    Bali Cycling Operator - Bali 131
    Adventure Cycling with Sobek - Bali 131
    Komune Resort & Beach Club - Bali 132
    Surf Goddess Retreats - Bali 134
  NIGHTLIFE IN BALI 135
    Old Man's 136
    Cocoon Beach Club - Bali 137
    No Mas Ubud 139
    40 Thieves 140
    La Favela - Bali 141
    Red Carpet Champagne Bar - Bali 142
    Rock Bar - Bali 143
    Pretty Poison 144
    UNIQUE Rooftop Bar Lounge & Restaurant - Bali 145
    Sky Garden - Bali 146
    Potato Head Beach Club - Bali 147
    Jenja - Bali 150
    Karma Beach - Karma Kandara 151

- Motel Mexicola - Bali 152
- Deus Cafe - Bali 153
- Metis Lounge - Bali 154
- Single Fin 155
- Double-Six Rooftop - Bali... 156

RESTAURANTS IN BALI 160
- Bridges 161
- Honzen Japanese Restaurant - Bali.............................. 162
- Bumbu Bali Restaurant and Cooking School - Bali 163
- Corner House - Bali 164
- Mama's German Restaurant - Bali 165
- Taco Casa - Seminyak - Bali 167
- Ultimo - Bali.. 167
- Meja Kitchen and Bar - Bali 168
- Sea Circus - Bali... 169
- Queens of India Ubud - Bali.. 171
- Dahana - Japanese Restaurant 172
- Taco Beach Grill - Bali... 172
- Mades Warung Seminyak - Bali 173
- Kayuputi Bali Fine Dining Restaurant - Bali 174
- Wacko Burger - Bali.. 175
- Drop. The Coffee Spot. - Bali 176
- Cafe des Artistes - Bali.. 177
- Chez Gado Gado - Bali.. 178
- Happy Chappy - Chinese Restaurant............................ 179
- Queens Tandoor Seminyak - Bali 181
- Sangkar Restaurant at the Bulgari - Bali....................... 183
- Taco Casa - Ubud - Bali... 184
- Cascades - Bali 185
- Revolver Espresso - Bali.. 186

WEDDINGS IN BALI 187
- Bali Good Food Catering - Bali 188
- Bali Elephant Safari Park Lodge - Bali........................... 189
- Bali Catering Company - Bali....................................... 191
- Bali Wedding Butler - Bali... 194

- P.T. Tirtha Bridal - Bali 199
- Jimbaran Puri Bali Weddings - Bali 204
- Mirage Chapel at Grand Mirage Resort - Bali 207
- Conrad Bali Weddings - Bali 210
- Dijon Bali Catering - Bali 215
- Simply Yours Wedding Caterers - Bali 218
- Heliconia Floral Art - Bali 220
- Courtyard Weddings at Nusa Dua - Bali 223
- Weddings at The Laguna Bali - Bali 225
- Westin Resort Wedding Planners - Bali 228
- The Beaded Boudoir - Bali 232
- Dini's Bridal - Bali 234
- Seventh Heaven Weddings - Bali 237
- Dominic Vanyi Artistic Photography - Bali 244
- Epic Photography - Bali 248
- Bali Limousine - Bali 248
- Bali Wedding Planners - Bali 251
- Weddings at The St Regis Bali Resort - Bali 258
- RUDYLIN Photography & Video Motion - Bali 260
- White Door Wedding Gallery - Bali 263
- Weddings at Ubud Hanging Gardens - Bali 265
- Wangi Bali Wedding Organizer and Co. - Bali 269
- Weddings at Ayana Resort and Spa Bali - Bali 274

Summary

The world is a book and those who do not travel read only one page.

It is indeed very unfortunate that some people feel traveling is a sheer waste of time, energy and money. Some also find traveling an extremely boring activity. Nevertheless, a good majority of people across the world prefer traveling, rather than staying inside the confined spaces of their homes. They love to explore new places, meet new people, and see things that they would not find in their homelands. It is this very popular attitude that has made tourism, one of the most profitable, commercial sectors in the world.

People travel for various reasons. Some travel for work, others for fun, and some for finding mental peace. Though every person may have his/her own reason to go on a journey, it is essential to note that traveling, in itself, has some inherent advantages. For one, for some days getting away from everyday routine is a pleasant change. It not only refreshes one's body, but also mind and soul. Traveling to a distant place and doing exciting things that are not thought of otherwise, can rejuvenate a person, who then returns home, ready to take on new and more difficult challenges in life and work. It makes a person forget his worries, problems, frustrations, and fears, albeit for some time. It gives him a chance to think wisely and constructively. Traveling also helps to heal; it can mend a broken heart.

For many people, traveling is a way to attain knowledge, and perhaps, a quest to find answers to their questions. For this, many people prefer to go to faraway and isolated places. For believers, it is a search for God and to gain higher knowledge; for others, it is a search for inner peace. They might or might not find what they are looking for, but such an experience certainly enriches their lives

David Mills

Introduction

Of the 18,000 islands under the Indonesian flag, only 6,000 are actually inhabited. This provides tourists with an exhaustive list of places to explore that are truly 'off the beaten path'. However, this doesn't mean travelers must be adventurous to enjoy a vacation to Indonesia, but it wouldn't be off the mark to suggest that Indonesia is Southeast Asia's most dynamic holiday destination.

Indonesia's stunning natural beauty is as diverse as the people that call the archipelago home. One of the most tectonically active nations on Earth, the area boasts a huge list of volcanoes to discover on dozens of different islands. Indonesia is also characterized by its abundance of coral cays and reefs, thick pockets of jungle, unique wildlife species and gorgeous beaches. Jungle trekking, scuba diving tours, boat cruises and hiking are just some activities visitors will come across in Indonesia.

The cities and towns of Indonesia are also worth visiting. Whether tourists want to explore the 'choppy' history of the country in the capital of Jakarta or shop for traditional handicrafts in Yogyakarta, there is something for everyone. For a more relaxed holiday experience, revelers should check out the thriving coastal communities of **Bali** to get their *Eat, Pray, Love* on at Kuta Beach and Legian Beach. The shopping, night life and relaxation in these areas are unmatched in Indonesia, and quite possibly the world.

Accommodation in Indonesia ranges from high-end and expensive five-star resorts, to extremely basic backpacker lodges. Some of the cheaper places do not meet the basic requirements of regular Western standards, such as private bathrooms or even running water so do your research before booking to avoid disappointment. On the other side of the spectrum, in places like Jakarta, Surabaya and Bali, some of Asia's most extravagant hotels can be found. Massage parlors and spas are a dime a dozen, and restaurants have a huge range of international cuisine for travelers. Nevertheless, Indonesian food in itself is so diverse that tourists are unlikely to get to experience everything.

Finding transportation to get around Indonesia is easy, but not always convenient. Domestic flights are reasonably cheap, but don't have the best safety record. Nevertheless, Garuda Air and Lion Air have started to develop a new carrier fleet, which is improving air networks. Inter-island ferry services are commonly used by locals and visitors, but can be overcrowded. In addition, rough seas during the rainy season are common. Despite some hassle, travelers won't have any trouble finding ways to get from one island to the next.

Buses are the main method of transportation between cities, although taxis can travel from one city to the next if they are in close proximity to each other. If car rental is selected, it would be better for tourists to rent a driver, too. Java and Sumatra boast rail services, which have been renovated in some areas since the Dutch constructed the network way back in the colonial era.

History

Early History of Indonesian Culture

For two millennia both Java and Bali have been in contact with India and neighbouring cultures, and this is clearly reflected in theatre and dance. Many of the remote islands, on the other hand, have lived in relative seclusion from outside influences, and have thus preserved traditions which, in some cases, stem from the Neolithic Stone Age or the Bronze Age. The island of Java was Islamised by the beginning of the 16th century, while the island of Bali has retained its old form of Hinduism to this day. Thus Bali has preserved its old culture, including several forms of theatre and dance. In Java the older Hindu-Buddhist traditions were adapted to the Islamic cultural atmosphere, resulting in the sophisticated court theatre and dance, discussed below.

"Several early Indianised kingdoms typical of South-East Asia flourished on the islands of Indonesia. The first of these was the Srivijaya maritime empire on the east coast of Sumatra, which controlled trade in the Malacca Straits from the 7th to the 13th centuries. Srivijayan dominance was also felt on the island of Java, where in the 8tth and 9th centuries the Mahayana Buddhist Shailendra dynasty and its contemporary, the Hindu Sanjaya dynasty, ruled. Since both competing dynasties flourished in the central parts of the island, this epoch, generally regarded as the "classical age" of Indonesian art and architecture, is known as the Central Javanese Period.

"At the beginning of the Central Javanese period, in the early 8th century AD, the region was ruled by the Buddhist Shailendra dynasty and the Hindu Sanjaya dynasty. Thus the area was divided into two cultural spheres. The Southern part was under Buddhist influence, while the Northern part was under Hindu control. From c. 830 onward the Hindu expansion was predominant, although there seems to have existed remarkable tolerance toward Buddhism. The Central Javanese period ended for reasons not exactly known, and the transfer of political power from Central Java to East Java took place from the 10th to the early 13th centuries.

Mataram (Medang) Culture

The Medang or Mataram Kingdom was a Javanese Hindu–Buddhist kingdom that flourished between the 8th and 10th centuries. It was based in Central Java, and later in East Java. Since the beginning of its formation, the Medang Mataram kings seemed to favour Shivaist Hinduism, such as the construction of Gunung Wukir Hindu temple as mentioned in Canggal inscription by king Sanjaya. However during the reign of Panangkaran and the rise of Sailendras influence, Mahayana Buddhism began to blossomed and gain court favour. The Kalasan, Sari, Mendut, Pawon and the magnificent Borobudur and Sewu temples testify the Buddhist renaissance in Central Java. The court patronage on Buddhism spanned from the reign of Panangkaran to Samaratungga. During the reign of Pikatan, Shivaist Hinduism began to regain court's favour, signified by the construction of grand Shivagrha (Prambanan).

The monumental Hindu temple of Prambanan in the vicinity of Yogyakarta initially built during the reign of King Pikatan (838 850), and expanded continuously through the reign of Lokapala (850 890) to Balitung (899–911) is a fine example of ancient Medang Mataram art and architecture. (See Below). Other Hindu temples dated from Medang Mataram Kingdom era are: Sambisari, Gebang, Barong, Ijo, and Morangan. Although the Shivaist regain the favour, Buddhist remain under royal patronage. The Sewu temple dedicated for Manjusri according to Kelurak inscription was probably initially built by Panangkaran, but later expanded and completed during Rakai Pikatan's rule, whom married to a Buddhist princess Pramod hawardhani, daughter of Samaratungga. Most of their subjects retained their old religion; Shivaist and Buddhist seems to co-exist in harmony. The buddhist temple of Plaosan, Banyunibo and Sajiwan were built during the reign of King Pikatan and Queen Pramodhawardhani, probably in the spirit of religious reconciliation after the battle of succession between Pikatan-Pramodhawardhani against Balaputra.

"From the 9th to mid 10th centuries, the Medang Kingdom witnessed the blossoming of art, culture and literature, mainly through the translation of Hindu-Buddhist sacred texts and the transmission and adaptation of Hindu-Buddhist ideas. The bas-relief narration of the Hindu epic Ramayana was carved on the wall of Prambanan Temple. During this period, the Kakawin Ramayana, an old Javanese rendering was written. This Kakawin Ramayana, also called the Yogesvara Ramayana, is attributed to the scribe

Yogesvara circa the 9th century CE, who was employed in the court of the Medang in Central Java. It has 2774 stanzas in the manipravala style, a mixture of Sanskrit and archaic Javanese prose. The most influential version of the Ramayana is the Ravanavadham of Bhatti, popularly known as Bhattikavya. The Javanese Ramayana differs markedly from the original Hindu. ><

The name of the Medang Kingdom was written in the Laguna Copperplate Inscription, dated 822 saka (900 CE), discovered in Manila, Philippines. The discovery of the inscriptions, written in the Kawi script in a variety of Old Malay containing numerous loanwords from Sanskrit and a few non-Malay vocabulary elements whose origin is ambiguous between Old Javanese and Old Tagalog, suggests that the people or officials of the Medang Kingdom had embarked on inter-insular trade and foreign relations in regions as far away as the Philippines, and that connections between ancient kingdoms in Indonesia and the Philippines existed.

Prambanan and Borobodur

Dr. Jukka O. Miettinen of the Theatre Academy Helsinki wrote: ""Central Javanese architecture shows a clear Indian influence. It is believed that Javanese temples or candies (ancient temples) were designed by learned Brahman priests and Buddhist monks, who acted as the scholars and scientists of their age and who either possessed the Indian architectural manuals or at least were familiar with them. The largest of all Central Javanese Hindu temples, and indeed of all Javanese Hindu temples, is the Loro Jonggaran group, also known as Prambanan. It was constructed in c. 835–856 and it comprises altogether 227 temple towers. The three main towers are dedicated to the Hindu trimurti of Shiva, Brahma and Vishnu. The central tower, dedicated to Shiva, rises to a height of 47 metres. The towers are decorated with narrative series of reliefs, which, in the temples dedicated to Shiva and Brahma, tell the story of the Ramayana. The exceptionally early Ramayana panels show few actual dance poses.

However, they include many fixed positions related to martial arts and archery. These poses and positions found their way into the later Javanese dance techniques.

"The largest Buddhist building is Borobodur, which, in fact, forms a huge three-dimensional mandala with a plan of 113 by 113 metres. Started in c. 775 its construction was intended to be a Hindu temple but later the plans were, however, changed and the Buddhist Borobudur got its final form in c. 835. The eight terraces of Bororobudur, with the crowning main stupa at the top surrounded by minor stupas, form an artificial stone mountain. The symbolism of Mount Meru, as well as other Buddhist cosmological features, is apparent. The lower terraces are built on a square plan symbolising the earth, whereas the upper terraces with stupas are circular and represent the heavens. The lower terraces were meant for circumambulation and were decorated with some 1300 relief panels of altogether 2.5 kilometres in length. As a whole, the structure forms a huge cosmological symbol and circumambulation through the terraces were intended to show the devotee, with the aid of the reliefs, the path to enlightenment.

Wayang Style of the East Javanese Period

Dr. Jukka O. Miettinen of the Theatre Academy Helsinki wrote: "From the early 10th century onward the Central Javanese kings focused their attention on East Java and in 929 they seem to have almost abandoned Central Java. There has been much speculation about the reason for this drastic change. A volcanic eruption could have been the reason, which was interpreted as a warning sign from the gods. The East Javanese period can be divided into four sub-periods.

The religion of the East Javanese period was syncretistic in character, while the cults of Shiva and the Buddha merged together. The free-standing cult images of the period do, in fact, follow the Central Javanese, Indian-influenced tradition. A more drastic change occurred, however, in the style of the narrative reliefs, which were carved on the bases and the balustrades of the outer walls of the temples. From the beginning of the 13th century they no longer echoed the Indian-influenced, round and sensual and even realistic "classical" style but were carved in a completely new style, known as the "wayang style".

"Wayang is a generic term, which has several meanings. It means a "puppet"; it can refer to a shadow and it also refers to a performance. Generally, the shadow play, wayang kulit, is seen as the origin of the whole "wayang family". It includes several theatrical genres from the storyteller's scroll performances, wayang beber, to the three-dimensional wooden rod puppet theatre, wayang golek, and finally to the court dance drama wayang wong, in which living actors take the place of the wayang puppets.

"All these theatre forms have much in common. Their principles of dramatic action, stylisation of movement, characterisation, costuming, basic role types etc. clearly stem from the same tradition and conventions. The earliest record confirming the existence of shadow theatre in Java dates back to 907. The present-day Balinese puppets represent an archaic style, and bear a clear resemblance to the East Javanese wayang style reliefs. The Javanese puppets are, in turn, believed to have evolved into their extremely elongated and almost non-figurative style during the period of Muslim rule, which put an end to the East Javanese period by the end of the 15th century. It is generally believed that the extreme stylisation of Javanese puppets reflects Islam's ban on making a human figure.

"Like the shadow puppets, especially those from Bali, the figures in the narrative panels of the East Javanese temples also follow the conventions of the wayang tradition. The torso is shown frontally, whereas the head, legs and feet are depicted in profile. The thin arms and small hands hang down stiffly alongside the torso if they are not lifted and shown in any of the wayang theatre's limited mudra-like gestures.

"The whole treatment of the reliefs is flat, while the large, decorative headdresses of the figures, the Chinese-style cloud motifs and the stylised elements of the landscape often fill the backgrounds. Besides the stylisation of the human figures, the dwarfish servant clowns, the punakawan, and the use of the tree-of-life motif as a dividing agent between the scenes also seem to connect the reliefs with the wayang kulit shadow theatre.

"The stories depicted in the East Javanese series of narrative reliefs are based on the localised versions of the Ramayana and other Indian mythological themes found in the Old Javanese texts. The stories that originated in India were, by this time, merged to a great extent with local stories and embedded in the local cultural climate. One can recognise a localisation process of the same kind both in the style of the reliefs as well as in the literary themes they depict.

"The mythological stories were retold and elaborated by local storytellers and court poets, while the sculptural portrayals of these stories were also localised. Thus the reliefs lost the style and iconography derived from India during the Central Javanese period, and a new completely indigenous wayang style emerged, indicating a cross-fertilisation of local theatrical conventions and the visual arts.

Majapahit Culture

During the Majapahit period, in the 13th–15th centuries, the East Javanese culture reached its zenith. The second half of the 14th century in particular saw the flourishing of both literature and architecture. The Nagarakertagama, written in 1365, depict a sophisticated court with refined taste in art and literature, and a complex system of religious rituals. The poet describes Majapahit as the centre of a huge mandala extending from New Guinea and Maluku to Sumatra and Malay Peninsula. Local traditions in many parts of Indonesia retain accounts in more or less legendary from 14th century Majapahit's power. Majapahit's direct administration did not extend beyond east Java and Bali, but challenges to Majapahit's claim to overlordship in outer islands drew forceful responses. +

Majapahit's writers continued the developments in literature and *wayang* (shadow puppetry) begun in the Kediri period. The best-known work today, Mpu Prapañca's *Desawarnaña*, often referred to as *Nāgarakertāgama*, composed in 1365, which provides us with an unusually detailed view of daily life in the kingdom's central provinces. Many other classic works also date from this period, including the famous Panji tales, popular romances based on the history of eastern Java that were loved and borrowed by storytellers as far away as Thailand and Cambodia. Many of Majapahit's administrative practices and laws governing trade were admired and later imitated elsewhere, even by fledgling powers seeking independence from Javanese imperial control.

"Negara Kertagama," by the famous Javanese author Prapancha (1335-1380) was written during this golden period of Majapahit, when many literary works were produced. Parts of the book described the diplomatic and economic ties between Majapahit and numerous Southeast Asian countries including Myanmar, Thailand, Tonkin, Annam, Kampuchea and even India and China. Other works in Kawi, the old Javanese language, were "Pararaton," "Arjuna Wiwaha," "Ramayana," and "Sarasa Muschaya." In modern times, these works were later translated into modern European languages for educational purposes.

The main event of the administrative calendar took place on the first day of the month of Caitra (March-April) when representatives from all territories paying tax or tribute to Majapahit came to the capital to pay court. Majapahit's territories were roughly divided into three types: the palace and its vicinity; the areas of east Java and Bali which were directly administered by officials appointed by the king; and the outer dependencies which enjoyed substantial internal autonomy.

The capital (Trowulan) was grand and known for its great annual festivities. Buddhism, Shaivism, and Vaishnavism were all practiced, and the king was regarded as the incarnation of the three. The Nagarakertagama does not mention Islam, but there were certainly Muslim courtiers by this time. Although brick had been used in the candi of Indonesia's classical age, it was Majapahit architects of the 14th and 15th centuries who mastered it. Making use of a vine sap and palm sugar mortar, their temples had a strong geometric quality.

A description of the Majapahit capital from the Old Javanese epic poem Nagarakertagama goes: "Of all the buildings, none lack pillars, bearing fine carvings and coloured" [Within the wall compounds] "there were elegant pavilions roofed with aren fibre, like the scene in a painting... The petals of the katangga were sprinkled over the roofs for they had fallen in the wind. The roofs were like maidens with flowers arranged in their hair, delighting those who saw them".

Impact of Islam on Indonesian Culture

Dr. Jukka O. Miettinen of the Theatre Academy Helsinki wrote: " Majapahit power gradually declined in the fifteenth century with the spread of Islam, and Malacca, the first of the South-East Asian sultanates, rose to power in the Malay Peninsula. Islam spread gradually from North Sumatra to Java, where Demak, the first Islamic centre, began to break away from Majapahit rule. In 1527, together with its neighbouring towns, it succeeded in crushing the Majapahit dynasty, bringing to an end the Hindu-Buddhist East Javanese period. According to legend, Islam was introduced into Java by nine holy men (wali). The most famous of these was Sunan Kali Jogo, who is believed to have spread the teachings of Islam by means of shadow-theatre performances of the Hindu Mahabharata. This legend clearly demonstrates the specific features of Islam in Java. Instead of wiping out earlier beliefs, it assimilated them.

"This led to a syncretistic belief system typical of Java, which combines animism, Buddhism, Hinduism, and Islam and has had a clear effect on the arts, including theatre and dance. As before, the ruler was regarded as divine, and the cult of the god-king and court culture retained many Hindu-Buddhist features of earlier times. Islam has not produced many forms of dance and theatre. The tradition of Islam (not Quran itself) takes a negative attitude towards portraying a human form in the visual arts. The only art form referred to in the Islamic tradition is the recitation of the holy Quran.

"When Islam started to spread across the islands of Indonesia in the 12th century, it was also bringing new kinds of cultural influences from the Islamic world, from Arab culture, Persia and Islamic West India. They included literature, types of instruments, forms of music, styles of recitation of holy texts, and also some forms of dance. In many cases these new elements were quickly localised and they intermingled with earlier animistic and Hindu-Buddhist elements. A good example is wayang golek rod puppet theatre, which has its roots firmly in the older wayang kulit shadow theatre that mainly deals with Hindu mythology. Wayang golek, however, takes its main plot material from the Islamic Menak stories. A similar kind of fusion of cultural layers can be recognised in numerous Indonesian traditions.

Malay-Islamic culture developed in Malacca (Melaka) a trading kingdom based on the Malay peninsula and the predominate power in Indonesia in the 15th century. Malacca's reign lasted little more than a century, but during this time it became the established centre of Malay culture. Malacca became a cultural centre, creating the matrix of the modern Malay culture: a blend of indigenous Malay and imported Indian, Chinese and Islamic elements. Malacca's fashions in literature, art, music, dance and dress, and the ornate titles of its royal court, came to be seen as the standard for all ethnic Malays. The court of Malacca also gave great prestige to the Malay language, which had originally evolved in Sumatra and been brought to Malacca at the time of its foundation. In time Malay came to be the official language of all the Malaysian states, although local languages survived in many places. After the fall of Malacca, the Sultanate of Brunei became the major centre of Islam.

"More purely Islamic traditions can be found on the island of Sumatra, particularly on its northernmost tip, Aceh, from where Islam started to spread to other parts of Indonesia. These traditions include, for example, certain musical styles, as well as dances, which are based on the local martial arts technique, silek. Forms of group dancing and singing (seudati and remplis mude) in which the formerly all-male cast use their own bodies to create music by singing, snapping their fingers and slapping their chests and legs are also popular. The lines sung are often religious texts, and it is believed that the tradition was inspired by the ecstatic rituals of the Muslim sufi mystics.

"After a period of dynastic warfare, the Mataram dynasty came to power, and Central Java again rose in political influence. One of the most important sultans of this dynasty was Agung (1613–1645), whose court in Yogyakarta ruled over the whole of East Java and other regions. Still existing dance forms as well as many mask and martial dances are known to have been performed at the court of Mataram."

Indonesian Culture During the Colonial Period

Dr. Jukka O. Miettinen of the Theatre Academy Helsinki wrote: "In the sixteenth century the island of Java had begun to interest Westerners who were seeking spices. In 1602 the Dutch established their trading company, the Vereenigde Oost-indische Compagnie, which led to a long period of Dutch hegemony on the islands of Indonesia. In 1619 the town of Batavia was founded at the site of the former village of Jayakarta. This miniature Amsterdam became a major port of trade and the centre of Dutch rule. The British were the main competitors in these areas, and they succeeded in acquiring dominance over Java from 1811 to 1816. After Dutch rule had been re-established, the actual colonial period began in 1830, when the Dutch gained control of the whole of Java.

"The Mataram dynasty expended its energies in the Javanese Wars of Succession. In 1755 the dynasty split into two, and two capitals, Yogyakarta (Yogya) and Surakarta (Solo), were founded only a few dozen kilometres from each other near the ancient Central Javanese temples. In both cities the most important part is the kraton (also known as keraton), the sultan's palace enclosed by walls and forming a city within a city.

"The symbolic features of the plan of the kraton clearly reflect ancient Hindu and Buddhist cosmology. The outermost parts of the kraton were reserved for the army and the court officials and their families. The interior consisted of several open administrative buildings serving various ceremonial functions. The sultan resided in the most protected central part, and, in accordance with old Hindu-Buddhist custom, he was regarded as divine.

"In the early nineteenth century the royal families of Yogyakarta and Surakarta again divided, leading to a politically precarious situation where the two capitals were simultaneously ruled by two sultans in each. When full political power was taken over by the Dutch, the ruling families of Java concentrated their energies on refining court etiquette and on developing the arts, especially theatre, dance, and music. This led to a unique renaissance of the arts, in which the classical genres of Central Javanese theatre and dance found their present forms."

In the early twentieth century, Europeans increasingly married across racial categories. In 1905 about 15 percent were in interracial marriages, rising to 27.5 percent by 1925. And, although by the mid-1920s the older mix of dress and sensibilities known as "Indies" (*Indische*) culture was rapidly giving way to more modern, urbanized, European- and American-influenced forms, numerous memoirs of Europeans, Eurasians, Chinese, and Indonesians make it clear that, despite obvious racial tensions and divisions, a new sort of Dutch-speaking, racially mixed, and culturally modern society was coming into being, mostly in the largest cities and mostly among the upper and upper-middle economic classes.

In smaller Indonesian cities, the heart of urban culture before the mid-twentieth century was a commercial sector surrounding a central square. The Dutch left a legacy of a basic civil architecture and street plans for large cities and towns in Java, Sumatra, and Bali, but after World War II most failed to experience a level of improved urban design and services commensurate with their tremendous population growth. Many cities, as a result, had minimal or makeshift services, with very simple sanitation, transportation facilities, and fire protection. Indonesian cities are internally segmented in complex, overlapping ways that differentiate ethnic groups, income levels, and professional specializations. Some older neighborhoods tend to house well-to-do business owners and high-level government officials, whereas other newer areas tend to be home to migrant communities from the rural areas. Some of these areas retain their system of close-knit social networks and are distinguished by the label kampung (village). However, the boundaries between one area and another are often unclear.

Indonesian Culture Under Sukarno anf Suharto

During the first 15 years of Indonesia's independent history there was remarkable flourishing of literature and painting that drew on the sense of personal and cultural liberation produced by the National Revolution. Dr. Jukka O. Miettinen of the Theatre Academy Helsinki wrote: "The rise of nationalism among Javanese intellectuals in the early twentieth century anticipated a period of political turmoil, which was later inflamed by World War II. After the end of the Japanese Occupation, Indonesia declared its independence. Yogyakarta was for a short time the temporary capital, and the seat of government was later moved to the Dutch-built city of Batavia, now renamed Jakarta. The Republic of Indonesia was established in 1950 with Dr A. Sukarno as its first elected president.

Worried about the invasion of foreign culture and Western music in particular, Sukarno introduced repressive legislation that encouraged artists and musicians to shun foreign influences and energize indigenous forms. These laws were repealed when Suharto came to power but did plant roots that allowed Indonesian culture to remain vital. In the Suharto years, the arts and culture was controlled to a large degree by the New Order government. The Information Ministry regulated all forms of media and banned more than 2,000 books.

Aubrey Belford of AFP wrote: "Suharto's personal quirks have also had an influence on Indonesian life. A Javanese man from the country's largest ethnic group, his error-laden and heavily accented version of the national language was imitated by sychophantic officials during his reign and leaked into wider usage, to the horror of purists. Although a Muslim, Suharto's devotion to traditional pre-Islamic mysticism also influenced the national culture. His Javanese brand of synchretic Islam, popularly known as Kejawen, later was added to the list of five major religions then recognised by the state, but under a different name: Belief in God Almighty...The supernatural still looms large especially when it comes to talk of the ex-dictator himself. While many would see Suharto's team of doctors as the main reason" he survived for so long while in poor health "theories popular among millions of Indonesians include possession by black magic and his ownership of a Javanese royal family's sacred dagger

The government of Indonesia saw itself as having a responsibility to advance a national culture throughout most of the New Order period, a project that was linked to requirements of national development and political integration. Government mandates aside, however, as more and more of the Indonesian population sought employment in large, poorly integrated cities consisting of diverse ethnic groups, the concept of a national culture had great appeal as a way of regulating these changing urban environments. Although the central government attempted to guide the formation of this culture through educational curricula, celebrations of national holidays, and careful control of the national media (popular art, television, and print media), this emerging culture came about only partly through central planning. Evidence of an emerging national culture also appeared in the far less controlled layout and social organization of cities; routines of social interaction using the official national language, Bahasa Indonesia; patterns of eating and preparing food; the viewing of team sports, such as soccer, badminton, and volleyball; movies and television programming; and material displays of wealth.

Culture Changes in Post-Suharto Indonesia

After Suharto was ousted the Information Ministry was abolished, books that were banned became available at bookstores and the *refomasi* movement took hold and brought new blood, and fresh irreverent ideas to the arts. A nation censorship board continued to exist but it was placed under the Culture Ministry and it operates with relatively little pressure from the government.

Abdurrahman Wahid, president of Indonesia from 1999 to 2001, was greatly revered as a brilliant scholar and cultured man. He advocated a tolerant and inclusive form of Islam and was known for his sense of humor, one-liners and pranks. He told dirty jokes to Clinton and posed beside a bust of Beethoven with a traditional Indonesian hat. Tom Fawthrop wrote in The Guardian, Wahid " Few countries have enjoyed a more cultured man at the helm of state a journalist, scholar and enlightened cleric, he took great delight in jazz and classical music and had a special passion for Beethoven. His wit was almost equal to his erudition. Upon losing the presidency in 2001, he quipped: "You don't realise that losing the presidency for me is nothing. I regret more the fact that I lost 27 recordings of Beethoven's Ninth Symphony."

Contemporary Indonesian public culture also provides some useful illustrations of how Indonesia has changed since Suharto was ousted. By mid-2009, after a comparatively short period of growth beginning around 2006, by far the most popular television genre in the nation was the reality show dating shows, talent contests, extreme home makeovers, and the like which are widely seen as being American in origin (although in fact British and Dutch producers were the true pioneers); nearly 80 different shows of this type were being produced by local companies. To both outsiders and many Indonesians, this seemed to be a sign of an abrupt change.

The Indonesian scholar and public intellectual Ariel Heryanto, for example, suggested that the pendulum had swung away from a post- 1998 interest in Islamic popular culture, and he talked about American culture being suddenly "in" among Indonesians at all economic and social levels. One reality-show producer even suggested that what viewers consider American values are in fact universal ones, and that Indonesians are now part of a world in which everyone shares "the same dream, no matter who you are and what nationality you are." Not surprisingly, some Western commentators took this as another confirmation that Indonesia had moved definitively into the liberal democratic camp.

There is an important "continuity" side to this story as well. For one thing, as New York Times reporter Norimitsu Onishi pointed out, the reality show is not the first American genre to attract attention. American sitcoms ranging from "I Love Lucy" to "The Golden Girls," as well as series such as "McGyver," filled Indonesian television schedules beginning in the mid-1970s but then lost ground to shows with Islamic themes and to telenovelas from Latin America and soap operas from Asia; the current fascination with televised reality shows is thus part of a longer evolution and should be interpreted in that light.

The careful foreign viewer might also notice that a number of the most popular Indonesian reality shows focus on themes markedly *not* found in America for example, transplanting wealthy or upper-middleclass Indonesians into poor, rural settings, and vice versa, focusing on the tribulations each group faces in making adjustments and attempting to understand an altogether different way of life. These productions tend to validate the values of modern, urban middle-class Indonesians at the same time as they highlight the importance of empathy for others, reflecting in part a longstanding mainstream nationalist populism and in part a Muslim morality and sensitivity to the plight of the poor. The analysis that the popularity of such reality shows is evidence of a recent and dramatic social change "Americanization," even is neither as accurate nor, truth be told, as interesting as the more complicated view that notices a more complex story of adaptation.

Culture and Arts in Indonesia

The arts especially painting, wood carving, dance, traditional music and puppetry are very much alive in Indonesia. In contrast to some Muslim countries, there are few objections to using representations of humans and animals in Indonesian art or for women to engage in dancing. The most well known art forms are produced in Java and Bali. *Alus* (refined) is a term used to describe the traditional Javanese appreciation of art. But the other islands have equally rich cultural traditions.

Simon Winchester wrote in the Wall Street Journal, "'When you arrive you cry; when you leave you cry."

This is a popular expatriate aphorism about India, but almost all who visit Indonesia for any time feel much the same. Arrival in Jakarta, the capital, is the worst. The pollution, the din, the ceaseless traffic. The garbage, the floods. Everything in those first few days is an assault. But then: Spend dawn on the top of Borobudur temple in central Java. The morning mist hugs the valleys; the rising sun spears shafts of gold between two great volcanoes; the ranks of Buddhas beside you are suddenly washed with a warm orange light, the figures becoming an army of the figures becoming an army of transcendent calm. Urban Indonesian nightlife centers on night markets, where people shop in toko (stores) and warung (food stalls). Also popular are forms of the performing arts such as pop music concerts, puppet shows, and the cinema.

Indonesia is culturally rich. Indonesian art and culture are intertwined with religion and age-old traditions from the time of early migrants with Western thoughts brought by Portuguese traders and Dutch colonists.

The basic principles which guide life include the concepts of mutual assistance or "gotong royong" and consultations or "musyawarah" to arrive at a consensus or "mufakat" Derived from rural life, this system is still very much in use in community life throughout the country.

Though the legal system is based on the old Dutch penal code, social life as well as the rites of passage are founded on customary or "adat" law which differs from area to area. "Adat" law has a binding impact on Indonesian life and it may be concluded that this law has been instrumental in maintaining equal rights for women in the community. Religious influences on the community are variously evident from island to island.
|+|

Intertwined with religion and age-old traditions from the time of early migrants the art and culture of Indonesia is rich in itself with Western thoughts brought by Portuguese traders and Dutch colonists. The art and culture of Indonesia has been shaped around its hundreds of ethnic groups, each with cultural differences that have shifted over the centuries. Modern-day Indonesian culture is a fusion of cultural aspects from Arabic, Chinese, Malay and European sources. Indonesian art and culture has also been influenced from the ancient trading routes between the Far East and the Middle East leading to many cultural practices being strongly influenced by a multitude of religions, including Hinduism, Buddhism, Confucianism and Islam.

"In music, in metropolitan Jakarta, the Java Jazz Festival is the annual meeting highlight for top international and Indonesian jazz musicians. Indonesia also boasts some of the best rock and pop bands and singers. Bands like Nidji, Ungu, Slang, Peter Pan and singing celebrities like Rossa, Agnes Monica, Kris Dayanti, Pasha, Ari Lasso, and many others, never fail to create a sensation wherever they appear in Indonesia as also in Malaysia and Singapore.

Diversity of Indonesia's Culture

Dr. Jukka O. Miettinen of the Theatre Academy Helsinki wrote: The Republic of Indonesia comprises 17 500 islands. With its estimated population of around 250 million people it is the world's fourth most populous country, and has the largest Muslim population in the world. Indonesia is a republic (since 1950 the Republic of Indonesia), with an elected legislature and a president. The nation's capital, Jakarta, is in Java, Indonesia's central island. The transcontinental country shares land borders with Papua New Guinea, East Timor and Malaysia. There are hundreds of theatrical traditions in Indonesia. Many of them belong to the smaller ethnic groups of remote islands while some of them form what could be classified as "classical traditions". These latter consist of the traditions of Indonesia's central island, Java, and the neighbouring, smaller island of Bali.

Indonesian culture and art reflects regional histories, relegions and influences of the archipelago's mind-boggling array of ethnic groups. Indonesia arts can be classified in to the three main streams within Indonesia. 1) The first, is that of the outer Indonesia, the islands of Sumatra, Kalimantan, Sulawesi, Sulawesi, Nusa Tenggara, Papua and Maluku, which have strong animist traditions. Carvings, weaving, pottery etc, have developed from a tribal art in which art objects are part of worship. 2) The second stream is that inner Indonesia, the islands of Java and Bali that have come under the greatest influence from Hindu-Budha tradition. The Technique and styles that built Borobudur and the Indian Epics such as The Mahabarata, that form the basis for wayang theatre are still a major influence in arts. 3) The third influences is that of Islam, which not so much introduced its own art & crafts traditions, but modified existing traditions.

Java, Indonesia's Cultural Heart

Dr. Jukka O. Miettinen of the Theatre Academy Helsinki wrote: "The long history of Java, the central island of Indonesia, is marked by international maritime contacts. The island is a natural crossroads of the sea routes between East and South Asia, and it has been the melting pot of cultural influences for thousands of years. This is clearly evident in the island's rich traditions of theatre and dance.

"The present classical forms of drama and dance were created by the Islamic courts of Central Java over the centuries. They combined old indigenous traditions with mythical story material and classical dance technique from India. Yogyakarta and Surakarta in Central Java and the capital, Jakarta, in the western part of the island are the main centres of Javanese dance and theatre today. **

"Java is also home to various classical forms of gamelan music and dance styles, of which the most important ones are the West Javanese style (Sunda), the East Javanese style, and the Central Javanese style, whose best-known traditions were refined in the kratons of Yogyakarta and Surakarta. The Central Javanese dance style can be described as the most classical dance style of Java. During the period of Indonesian independence the dance style of Java and its theatre traditions have spread to other islands, forming a kind of pan-Indonesian style. **

"For over a thousand years, wayang kulit shadow theatre has been the core of Javanese theatre, influencing the development of other genres. Over the centuries, the various sultanates with their kraton have developed their own art forms by adapting and combining ancient Hindu-Buddhist traditions in the spirit of Islam. **

Traditional Culture of Indonesia

Halus (refined) Javanese culture still exits. Rooted in Hinduism, it revolves around respect for the sultan and appreciation of the high culture and arts that are associated with it. Sultans particularly those in

Yogyakarta and Solo have traditionally presided over Muslim rituals and served as unifying symbols. They have been regarded as the focal points for art forms such as painting, batik. music and masked dance. Sultans are known officially as "Susunan" the "Volcano" or 'Life-Giving Mountain," Every year the Sultan of Yogyakarta throws an offering of his hair and fingernail clippings into Merapi volcano.

In 2009, UNESCO recognized Indonesia's "Batik" as a World Intangible Cultural Heritage, adding to the earlier recognized Indonesia's "Keris" (the wavy blade dagger), and the "Wayang" shadow puppets. Further being considered as World Heritage is the "Angklung" bamboo musical instrument from West Java, being uniquely "Indonesian".

The Indonesian archipelago harbours many ancient cultures that are rooted here, while throughout its history through centuries until today the islands have been influenced by Indian, Chinese, Arabic and European cultures, and lately also by the global popular culture, international travel and internet. Foreign cultures and traditions, however, are absorbed and assimilated by the people producing unique "Indonesian" creations found nowhere else in the world.

Indonesia's culture is indeed rich in the arts and crafts. In textiles, Sumatra produces some of the best gold and silver-thread woven sarongs, known as songket; South Sulawesi women produce colourful hand-woven silks, while Bali, Flores and Timor produce some of the best textiles from natural fibers using complicated motifs. In wood craft, Bali's artisans produce beautiful sculptures, as do the Asmat in Papua, both traditional and modern, Central Java's craftsmen produce finely carved furniture, while Bugis shipbuilders of South Sulawesi continue to build the majestic "phinisi" schooners that ply the Indonesian seas until today.

Indonesia is also strong in the performing arts. The beautiful Ramayana dance drama is enacted during the dry season at the large open stage at Prambanan near

Yogyakarta under a tropical full moon and against the dramatic illuminated background of this 9th.century temple. Indonesia's dances are colourful, dramatic or entertaining. They vary from the highly synchronized "saman" song and dance from Aceh, to the sedate and sophisticated court dances from Java accompanied by the liquid sounds of the gamelan orchestra, to the war dances of Kalimantan, Papua, and Sulawesi. Chinese influence can be seen along the entire north coast of Java from the batik patterns of Cirebon and Pekalongan, to the finely carved furniture and doors of Kudus in Central Java, as also in the intricate gold embroidered wedding costumes of West Sumatra.

Support for the Arts

In the past in Java and Bali, royal courts or rich persons were major patrons of the arts. They continue their support, but other institutions joined them. The Dutch founded the Batavia Society for the Arts and Sciences in 1778, which established the National Museum that continues to display artifacts of the national culture. The Dutch-founded National Archive seeks to preserve the literary heritage, despite poor funding and the hazards of tropical weather and insects. Over the past several decades, regional cultural museums were built using national and provincial government funding and some foreign aid. Preservation of art and craft traditions and objects, such as house architecture, batik and tie-dye weaving, wood carving, silver and gold working, statuary, puppets, and basketry, are under threat from the international arts and crafts market, local demands for cash, and changing indigenous values.

A college for art teachers, founded in 1947, was incorporated in 1951 into the Technological Institute of Bandung; an Academy of Fine Arts was established in Yogyakarta in 1950; and the Jakarta Institute of Art Education was begun in 1968. Academies have since been founded elsewhere; the arts are part of various universities and teacher training institutes; and private schools for music and dance have been founded. Private galleries for painters and batik designers are legion in Yogyakarta and Jakarta. Academies and institutes maintain traditional arts as well as develop newer forms of theater, music, and dance. [Ibid]

Culture Wars Between Indonesia and Malaysia

Simon Winchester wrote in the Wall Street Journal, ""Culture wars" also were underway. In a series of disputes with neighboring Malaysia over traditional cultural heritage, public voicesmany on the Internet became surprisingly shrill, including characterizations of Malaysia as "a nation of thieves," and threats of war. In mid2009, a Malaysian Ministry of Tourism advertisement aired internationally on the Discovery Channel portrayed a Balinese dance as part of Malaysia's cultural heritage; the government subsequently withdrew the advertisement and apologized for what it said had been a production error. But the uproar nevertheless gathered steam, and by September, despite some Indonesian commentators' dismissal of the issue as trivial and an indication of Indonesian feelings of inferiority, it had become a cause célèbre threatening diplomatic relations. Some of the sharp feelings on the Indonesian side were apparently assuaged in October when the United Nations Educational, Scientific, and Cultural Organization (UNESCO) declared batik to be part of Indonesia's intangible cultural heritage, adding to a similar declaration in 2008 for shadow puppet theater (*wayang kulit*) and the *keris*, an asymmetrical dagger, which many Malaysians had felt were at least equally theirs.

Cultural War Between Malaysia and Indonesia

John M. Glionna wrote in the Los Angeles Times, " For decades, Uni Histayanti has performed the enigmatic movements of her country's traditional pendet dance.

She learned the rhythms as an infant and years ago opened a dinner theater in Jakarta where, dressed in native costume, she performs nightly. As she flutters her arms bird-like, darts her eyes and tilts her head at exotic angles, she invokes the welcoming spirit of the Hindu-majority Bali island where it originated centuries ago. That's why it floored her to hear that neighboring Malaysia had reportedly tried to seize the pendet as its own. It's pure cultural piracy, Histayanti insists. And it makes her mad. "It's a symbol of our heritage, not theirs," she said as she applied makeup in a backstage dressing room of her theater. "If you have something and someone tries to steal it, you take it back."

"These two predominantly Muslim neighbors, which share ethnic and physical traits, are engaged in a tense struggle for superiority. Nowadays, the rift is widening. It's cultural. It's political. And recently, it has gotten personal. Many Malaysians dismiss the teeming Indonesian archipelago as a source for the low-class maids, parking-lot jockeys and waiters who work in

Kuala Lumpur and other cities in Malaysia. For their part, Indonesians icily counter that Malaysia is so desperate for a culture that it will resort to anything even outright theft to acquire one.

"The pendet dance tiff is only one example of battle over so-called proprietary traditions. "A fresh skirmish of the culture wars breaks out now and then when Indonesians claim Malaysians have yet again plagiarized their indigenous art and music. Malaysians have reportedly laid claim to the Indonesian reog performances a mix of dance and magic, as well as the angklung, a bamboo musical instrument, activists say. In 2007, Indonesia threatened legal action against Malaysia for allegedly co-opting Indonesian songs and dances in its national tourism campaign. That resulted in a high-profile panel being convened to settle the dispute.

"Many in Indonesia claim that even Malaysia's national anthem borrows from an Indonesian song. Experts solicited to settle the fight reported that both songs borrow from a 19th century French tune. At home, many Indonesians say, Malaysians are protective of their own culture. When a wave of Indonesian pop music began receiving play on radio stations there a year ago, officials sought to set a strict quota: 90 percent Malaysian songs and 10 percent Indonesian."

Cultural War Between Malaysia and Indonesia Get Ugly

John M. Glionna wrote in the Los Angeles Times, ""The pendet dance tiff emerged in the summer of 2009 when rumors spread that Malaysia was responsible for television ads claiming the invention of the pendet dance. Within days, a private company producing a program for the Discovery Channel admitted they were behind the ads and that they had mistakenly picked the wrong dance to promote their upcoming program. The Malaysian government, they explained, had nothing to do with the foul-up."

"But it was too late. Indonesia's feathers had been ruffled. Indonesia's tourism minister demanded a written apology, which he said was needed for the record. Meanwhile, outraged Indonesians waged a "Crush Malaysia" campaign reminiscent of a nationalistic tirade in the 1960s. This time, mobs burned the Malaysian flag, which features a crescent moon and sun, and threw rotten eggs at the embassy in Jakarta.

"For days, protesters wielding sharpened bamboo sticks stopped traffic in search of Malaysian motorists and pedestrians. Six Indonesians were arrested. No one was injured, but the Malaysian Embassy complained about the safety of its citizens. Internet hackers attacked Malaysian government websites. One nationalist youth group began collecting signatures on the Internet for volunteers willing to go to war with Malaysia. Though the leaders of the youth group concede that such a face-off is extremely unlikely, they say they have stockpiled food, medicine and weapons such as samurai swords and ninja throwing-stars."

The Straits Times reported: "The curious tiff between Malaysia and Indonesia defies rationality. Vigilante gangs in Indonesia have sought to "sweep" Malaysians out at roadblocks. Protesters have pelted the Malaysian embassy with bad eggs. These came about after Indonesians accused Malaysians of hijacking a Balinese dance for a promotional campaign on Malaysia. The affair is doubly irrational when one considers the fact that the error was committed not by Malaysia but by the widely watched cable Discovery Channel.

Bitter Feelings Behind the Cultural War Between Malaysia and Indonesia

John M. Glionna wrote in the Los Angeles Times, "Such high jinks baffle many Malaysians, not to mention Indonesians."These guys with pointed sticks, they're from the loony left," said Ong Hock Chuan, a Malaysian-born public relations consultant who lives in Jakarta. "If it wasn't Malaysia, they'd vent their anger at something else." But many others here say the resentment is widespread and runs deep. Newspapers run stories about mistreatment of some of the 2 million Indonesian workers by their bosses in Malaysia. Last year, Indonesia temporarily stopped sending maids to Malaysia until better security was provided for the workers.

"Many who want to invade Malaysia are former migrant workers or people who know one," said Aleksius Jemadu, a political scientist at Pelita Harapan University in Indonesia. "There is a sense that Malaysians look down on us. They insult us. And to tell you the truth, many Indonesians are secretly envious because they view most Malaysians as being better off than us." The two governments also remain at loggerheads. "Each wants to be seen as the regional leader in Southeast Asia," he said. "They both claim to be the leading Muslim nation."

"The vitriol and bad feelings spill over into politics. Animosity rose this summer after two Jakarta hotels were bombed, an attack apparently planned by a Malaysian citizen linked to Al Qaeda, Noordin Mohammad Top, who was later killed. Ong, the Malaysian Indonesian consultant, writes on his blog that Indonesians should be angry at their own government "for doing so little to capitalize on their culture, which is varied and rich beyond description, and hence letting great opportunities slip away." But Ong says there is much blame to go around. The Malaysian government, he says, "needs to get off its high horse" and treat Indonesian officials as equals. For now, Histayanti says, she will continue to perform the pendet dance for all her customers even Malaysians. "I feel sorry for them," she said. "They're just jealous of us."

The Straits Times reported: " Malaysia has progressed much faster than Indonesia and jobs are more plentiful than could be created in Indonesia for its much bigger population. The economic gap has resulted in a flood of surplus Indonesian workers into Malaysia to do '3D' (dirty, dangerous and demeaning) jobs in sectors such as construction, plantations and household help. Against this backdrop, ordinary Indonesians rile against being treated as second-class by their kinsmen. Some insensitive Malaysians exacerbate matters when they assert their position in the superior-subordinate relationship. The curious tiff between Malaysia and Indonesia defies rationality. Vigilante gangs in Indonesia have sought to "sweep" Malaysians out at roadblocks.

"Both countries would do well to stress their common and shared cultural heritage, rather than allow their citizens to score nationalist points by declaring exclusive ownership of cultural symbols. As one Malaysian minister has noted, India did not make any noise about Hindi songs being sung in Malaysia and Indonesia. (To buttress the point, India has also never protested against the use of its great Ramayana and Mahabharata epics in Indonesia's wayang kulit.)

Indonesian Literature

Indonesia has created many celebrated authors. There has also been a long tradition, particularly among ethnically Malay populations, of impromptu, interactive, verbal composition of poetry referred to as the 'pantun'. There is a long Javanese tradition of the poet as a "voice on the wind," a critic of authority. During the Suharto era, poets and playwrights had works banned, among them W. S. Rendra whose plays were not allowed in Jakarta. Pramoedya Ananta Toer, a well-known author won the Magsaysay Award and was considered for the Nobel Prize in Literature.

Indonesia's literary legacy includes centuries-old palm, bamboo, and other fiber manuscripts from several literate peoples, such as the Malay, Javanese, Balinese,

Buginese, Rejang, and Batak. The fourteenth century Nagarakrtagama is a lengthy poem praising King Hayam Wuruk and describing the life and social structure of his kingdom, Majapahit. The I La Galigo of the Bugis, which traces the adventures of their culture hero, Sawerigading, is one of the world's longest epic poems.

Although the culture of India, largely embodied in insular Southeast Asia with the Sanskrit language and the Hindu and Buddhist religions, was eagerly grasped by the elite of the existing society, typically Indian concepts, such as caste and the inferior status of women, appear to have made little or no headway against existing Indonesian traditions. Nowhere was Indian civilization accepted without change; rather, the more elaborate Indian religious forms and linguistic terminology were used to refine and clothe indigenous concepts. In Java even these external forms of Indian origin were transformed into distinctively Indonesian shapes. The tradition of plays using Javanese shadow puppets (wayang), the origins of which may date to the neolithic age, was brought to a new level of sophistication in portraying complex Hindu dramas (lakon) during the period of Indianization. Even later Islam which forsakes pictorial representations of human brings, brought new developments to the wayang tradition through numerous refinements in the sixteenth to eighteenth centuries.

The Javanese has a literary history dating back to the 8th century. Many of their folk stories are based on Hindu stories from India. During the Medang or Mataram Kingdom a Javanese Hindu–Buddhist kingdom that flourished between the 8th and 10th centuries in Central Java, and later in East Java there was blossoming of art, culture and literature, mainly through the translation of Hindu-Buddhist sacred texts and the transmission and adaptation of Hindu-Buddhist ideas. The bas-relief narration of the Hindu epic Ramayana was carved on the wall of Prambanan Temple. During this period, the Kakawin Ramayana, an old Javanese rendering was written. This Kakawin Ramayana, also called the Yogesvara Ramayana, is attributed to the scribe Yogesvara circa the 9th century CE, who was employed in the court of the Medang in Central Java. It has 2774 stanzas in the manipravala style, a mixture of Sanskrit and archaic Javanese prose. The most influential version of the Ramayana is the Ravanavadham of Bhatti, popularly known as Bhattikavya. The Javanese Ramayana differs markedly from the original Hindu.

"When Islam started to spread across the islands of Indonesia in the 12th century, it was also bringing new kinds of cultural influences from the Islamic world, from Arab culture, Persia and Islamic West India. They included literature, types of instruments, forms of music, styles of recitation of holy texts, and also some forms of dance. In many cases these new elements were quickly localised and they intermingled with earlier animistic and Hindu-Buddhist elements. A good example is wayang golek rod puppet theatre, which has its roots firmly in the older wayang kulit shadow theatre that mainly deals with Hindu mythology. Wayang golek, however, takes its main plot material from the Islamic Menak stories. A similar kind of fusion of cultural layers can be recognised in numerous Indonesian traditions. **

Majapahit Literature and the Nagarakertagama

During the Majapahit period, in the 13th–15th centuries, the East Javanese culture reached its zenith. The second half of the 14th century in particular saw the flourishing of both literature and architecture. Majapahit's writers continued the developments in literature and *wayang* (shadow puppetry) begun in the Kediri period. The best-known work today, Mpu Prapañca's *Desawarnaña*, often referred to as *Nāgarakertāgama*, composed in 1365, which provides us with an unusually detailed view of daily life in the kingdom's central provinces. Many other classic works also date from this period, including the famous Panji tales, popular romances based on the history of eastern Java that were loved and borrowed by storytellers as far away as Thailand and Cambodia. Many of Majapahit's administrative practices and laws governing trade were admired and later imitated elsewhere, even by fledgling powers seeking independence from Javanese imperial control.

"Negara Kertagama," by the famous Javanese author Prapancha (1335-1380) was written during this golden period of Majapahit, when many literary works were produced. Parts of the book described the diplomatic and economic ties between Majapahit and numerous Southeast Asian countries including Myanmar, Thailand, Tonkin, Annam, Kampuchea and even India and China. Other works in Kawi, the old Javanese language, were "Pararaton," "Arjuna Wiwaha," "Ramayana," and "Sarasa Muschaya." In modern times, these works were later translated into modern European languages for educational purposes.

A description of the Majapahit capital from the Old Javanese epic poem Nagarakertagama goes: "Of all the buildings, none lack pillars, bearing fine carvings and coloured" [Within the wall compounds] "there were elegant pavilions roofed with aren fibre, like the scene in a painting... The petals of the katangga were sprinkled over the roofs for they had fallen in the wind. The roofs were like maidens with flowers arranged in their hair, delighting those who saw them".

Literature from the Dutch Period in Indonesia

In colonial times some literature was published in regional languages, the most being in Javanese, but this was stopped after Indonesian independence. The earliest official publishing house for Indonesian literature is Balai Pustaka, founded in Batavia in 1917. National culture was expressed and, in some ways formed, through spoken Malay-Indonesian (understood by many people) and newspapers, pamphlets, poetry, novels, and short stories for those who could read.

The literature on Dutch expansion and the Netherlands East Indies is extensive. The most comprehensive work on the Cultivation System is perhaps Robert E. Elson's Village Java under the Cultivation System. The 1860 novel Max Havelaar: Or the Coffee Auctions of the Dutch Trading Company by Multatuli, penname of Eduard Douwes Dekker, is still captivating reading. It w as polemic against injustice by Dutch colonist in Java in the 1850s. A History of Modern Indonesia by Adrian Vickers begins its coverage with the late nineteenth century, and the collection of papers edited by Robert B. Cribb in The Late Colonial State in Indonesia is very useful. *

Modern Literature in Indonesia

Modern Indonesian literature got its start with language unification efforts in 1928 and underwent considerable development before the war, receiving further impetus under Japanese auspices. Revolutionary (or traditional) Indonesian themes were employed in drama, films, and art, and hated symbols of Dutch imperial control were swept away.

Michael J. Ybarra wrote in the Los Angeles Times, "Indonesia is one of the world's largest countries, but it's also a relatively young one. When the Indonesian republic was born in 1949, after three centuries of Dutch colonialism, language was one forge of nationalism. The new country stretched from the Indian Ocean to the Pacific, encompassing 17,000 islands. The archipelago was also a riot of languages with some 300 tongues spoken. The literary tradition was more oral than written, everything from the spoken word epics of the Kalimantan Dayaks in Borneo to Javanese court songs. The new government declared Bahasa Indonesia (a dialect of Malay) the national language. "Indonesia owes its identity to the Indonesian language," says novelist Pramoedya Ananta Toer.

By the time of independence, literary production was not great, but it has grown considerably since the 1950s. The literary tradition is now rich, but one should note that reading for pleasure or enlightenment is not yet part of the culture of average urban Indonesians and plays little if any part in the life of village people. Indonesia has made literacy and widespread elementary education a major effort of the nation, but in many rural parts of the country functional literacy is limited. For students to own many books is not common; universities are still oriented toward lecture notes rather than student reading; and libraries are poorly stocked.

Modern Writers and Books in Indonesia

In the conflict between left-and right-wing politics of the 1950s and early 1960s, organizations of authors were drawn into the fray. In the anticommunist purges of the late 1960s, some writers who had participated in left-wing organizations were imprisoned. The most famous is Pramoedya Ananta Toer, a nationalist who had also been imprisoned by the Dutch from 1947 to 1949. He composed books as stories told to fellow prisoners in exile on the island of Buru from 1965 to 1979. He was released from Buru and settled in Jakarta, but remained under city arrest. Four of his novels, the Buru Quartet, published between 1980 and 1988 in Indonesian, are rich documentaries of life in turn-of-the-century colonial Java. They were banned in Indonesia during the New Order. Pram (as he is commonly known, rhyming with Tom) received a PEN Freedom-to-Write Award in 1988 and a Magsaysay Award in 1995. In English translation, the Buru Quartet received critical acclaim, and after the end of the New Order in 1999, Pram made a tour of the United States. He is the only Indonesian novelist to have received such acclaim overseas.

Famous writers and intellectuals include: W. S. Rendra, major poet and playwright who achieved fame during the New Order for taking stands against the government; Akhdiat Miharja, a key figure in literature during the 1940s and 1950s; Des Alwi, one of the last figures of the revolutionary period (he was the adopted son of Mohammad Hatta and a close associate of Sutan Syahrir), and later diplomat and writer; and Rosihan Anwar, legendary reporter, columnist, and public intellectual. Chairil Anwar was also an important figure in the literature world and a member of the Generation 45 group of authors who were active in the Indonesian independence movement.

Some well known Indonesian writers set their stories in fantasy words. Others have used the Dutch period to criticize the Sukarno and Suharto eras. *The Dancer* by Ahmad Tohari was banned under Suharto. It was about village life during the massacre in the 1860s. It paints an unflattering picture of the military. Mochtar Lubis is another highly regarded Indonesian writer. His most well known novel, *Twilight in Jakarta*, examines corruption and the problems of the poor in 1950s Jakarta. This book too was banned and Lubis was jailed. Fira Basuki wrote the trilogy *Jendala-Jendala* ("The Windows"), *Pintu* ("The Door") and *Atap* ("The Roof"). Dew Lestari is a singer who wrote the popular novel *Supernova*.

Lack of English Translations and Interest in Indonesian Literature

Michael J. Ybarra wrote in the Los Angeles Times, "In 1986 the king of Thailand gave an award to Indonesian poet Sapardi Djoko Damono for his contributions to Indonesia's literature. Damono, in turn, wanted to hand out some of his verse when he accepted the award in Bangkok. The only problem was Damono's work had never been translated into another language. So the poet asked his friend John McGlynn to prepare a selection in English, the lingua franca of Southeast Asia. For McGlynn, an American translator living in Jakarta, it was a flashback to when he started studying the

Indonesian language in college a decade earlier. "It was ridiculous," he says. "I had studied Japanese and Chinese literature in translation, but for Indonesian there were less than five books in translation."

"Indonesia's great writer Pramoedya Ananta Toer said, "A translated book is more important than a diplomat." McGlynn concurs. "Before Lontar there was no possibility of teaching Indonesia literature abroad, of finding out aspects of Indonesian culture beyond politics or economics," he says. "I want people to understand the Indonesia I care about. My passion is for Indonesia more than Indonesian literature, but I do feel that only through arts and culture can you understand another culture."

"It was puppets, not books, that first brought McGlynn to Indonesia. A theater major from the University of Wisconsin, McGlynn came to Indonesia in 1976 to study wayang kulit, the famous shadow puppet theater. He had begun studying the language in Wisconsin and continued at the University of Indonesia in Jakarta. His interest in puppets waned as he began to learn about the country's literature. "At first, literature was only a tool to learn the language," he says. "I asked my professor to set up a course to study Indonesian literature. I was the only student. I wasn't truly viewing it as literature. I wanted a greater understanding of the culture. Then I found a lot of gems. It was only after a few years that I got a calling, a mission."

"McGlynn returned to the U.S. long enough to earn a master's at the University of Michigan in 1981. "I think it was the first degree in Indonesian literature in the U.S.," he says. Over the last two decades some 20 American universities have added the teaching of Indonesian literature, usually under the auspices of Southeast Asian studies (the topic is more popular in Australia).

"Even in Indonesia the country's literature is not exactly a priority. "English is a mandatory subject in school," McGlynn says. "Indonesian literature is not."

Lontar Executive Director Adila Suwarno said, "I'm Indonesian, but I'm disappointed there are not many Indonesians that realize how important it is to preserve our culture. But I understand that. A country like ours has to feed and house people first. It's easier to collect funding for poverty. This is too sophisticated.""

Effort to Get Indonesian Literature Translated to English

Michael J. Ybarra wrote in the Los Angeles Times, "McGlynn, along with Damono and several other Indonesian writers, McGlynn formed an organization to translate and promote the largely unknown literature from the world's fourth most populous nation. In 1988 the Lontar Foundation was born; its first publication was a collection of Damono's work called "Suddenly the Night." Since then the foundation has published scores of books and branched out into documenting some of the archipelago's cultural traditions, such as regional theater and dance, which are threatened by the irresistible pull of globalization. "Until Lontar was established, people abroad didn't look at Indonesian literature as literature," McGlynn says. "Whenever Indonesia appears in a newspaper it's because of a disaster. I wanted to create a more accurate picture. Not necessarily a better picture but a more balanced one."

"Professor Hendrik Maier, an expert on Malay literature who teaches in the new Southeast Asian studies program at UC Riverside, agrees that the foundation has made the study of Indonesian writing possible in the English-speaking world. "Lontar made a lot of things accessible in good translations," he says. "At last we have these books in English. It's also good for the self-confidence of the Indonesians; they're proud that they get their place in the world."

"The idea for Lontar, McGlynn says, came from an Indian organization called the Seagull Foundation that was formed in 1987 to promote South Asian arts. The name Lontar refers to the palm-leaf manuscripts that record the archipelago's oldest writing. For the first several years, McGlynn and the other staff worked for free. McGlynn earned his living by translating Indonesian economic journals into English. Today, Lontar employs 25 people, has its own website (www.lontar.org) and operates on an annual budget of about $100,000. McGlynn is the director of publications. About a third of the foundation's revenue comes from publishing, another third from the sale of note cards and calendar reproductions of beautiful illustrated manuscripts. The rest comes from donors such as the Ford Foundation and the Luce Foundation.

"Lontar has published 40 books. The titles don't exactly have bestseller written all over them: There's a four-volume history of Indonesian theater, a six-volume collection of Javanese literature, an oral history from survivors of the bloody anti-communist purge of the 1960s, the first history of Indonesian cinema and a boxed set of bilingual theater texts. After Sept. 11, Lontar put out a volume called "Manhattan Sonnet," which featured prose and poetry by 24 Indonesian writers who had lived in New York or traveled in the U.S. "We want to distribute more aggressively to schools around the world," Suwarno says. "Our educational system is terrible. In our small world we need information for Indonesian students."

"Lontar is also preserving other aspects of the country's culture with a series of films, ranging from interviews with writers such as Toer and Damono to Balinese shadow puppet performances. The foundation also houses a library stuffed with rare books, old photographs, slides of manuscripts and performances. "Our mission is to promote Indonesia through literature," Suwarno says. "I really hope we become one of the biggest libraries of information in Indonesia that everyone will be able to access. It's a long-term project.

Saman, Ayu Utami and Sex

The most talked about book in Indonesia in the 1990s was *Saman*, a novella by an unknown 27-year-old woman named Ayu Utami. The book was a success because it dealt with subjects that until that time had been taboo: political, repression, prejudice towards the Chinese, and premarital sex. An American writer based in Jakarta told the International Herald Tribune, "That book was a whirlwind. No one had talked about politics like that before, or, for that matter, about sex like that before."

The story is about a Catholic priest and his relationship with four former female students, one of whom he has a sexual affair with. Other characters include Christian Chinese, political activists and a rubber tapper. The description of the sex scenes involving the priest are quite graphic, especially by Indonesian standards.

Utami herself is a Catholic, who was born in 1960 and grew up in Bogor, near Jakarta. She worked as a journalist until she was fired in 1994 for working with an anti-Suharto group called the Association of

Independent Journalists. She also wrote *Larung* and*Sex, Sketches and Stories* and cites the Bible as an early inspiration.

"Saman" was published two weeks before Suharto's fall. Newsweek reported: "Set during his oppressive regime, the novel raised eyebrows mainly for touching on both religious and sexual matters: the main character has an affair with a Catholic priest. Drawing skillfully on both Indonesian slang and literary allegory, "Saman" won the prestigious Jakarta Arts Council competition for new novels and quickly went on to sell 55,000 copies--a good run in Indonesia.

After the release of Sex, Sketches and Stories, Peter Janssen wrote in Newsweek, "At the dimly lit Sudirman International Cafe, the literati have gathered to drink beer, smoke cigarettes and listen to a young woman talk about sex. The scene wouldn't be notable in most cities, but this is Jakarta, capital of the world's most populous Muslim country. Ayu Utami, 35, a slender Javanese beauty with sharp features and an open smile, is launching her newest book, a collection of essays entitled "Sex, Sketches and Stories." Sporting a skintight top, Utami deftly fields questions on such topics as marriage, infidelity and sexual liberation. "People think of free sex as something done by people who aren't married, but actually free sex is something done by married people," says Utami to shouts of approval. "I love you!" yells one young woman, hoisting a beer. "

Sastra wangi: Indonesia's Sexy Feminist Literary Movement

Ayu Utami and her 1998 novel Saman is noted as starting the sastra wangi movement Sastra wangi (also spelled sastrawangi; literally, "fragrant literature") is a label given to a new body of Indonesian literature written by young, urban Indonesian women who take on controversial issues such as politics, religion and sexuality. The controversial label "sastra wangi" originated among predominantly male critics in the early 2000s to categorize such young, female writers as Ayu Utami, Dewi Lestari, Fira Basuki and Djenar Maesa Ayu. Utamis said, "There's always a tendency to categorize literary work, and sastra wangi is one such category ... The media came up with [the name] because we weren't the typical writers who used to lead the local literary scene. Beyond that, I don't know the meaning or significance of sastra wangi."

Peter Janssen wrote in Newsweek, "Since the downfall of the autocratic President Suharto five years ago, Indonesia has undergone plenty of upheaval: three presidents, innumerable riots and demonstrations, bloody sectarian clashes between Muslims and Christians. Far less noticed has been the rise of provocative Indonesian literature, thanks largely to a group of bright, bold, attractive, media-savvy young women who are willing to take on the subject of sex. Their growing body of work has been lumped under the label sastra wangi--literally, "fragrant literature"--a somewhat derogatory term that has nonetheless stuck and helped the movement catch on. "There is a newfound freedom now," says Richard Oh, owner of the QB World Book chain. "These writers aren't afraid to say anything. This is the first new trend in Indonesian literature for ages and ages."

Utami launched the movement with her first novel, "Saman," two weeks before Suharto's fall. "A succession of women writers quickly followed, each pushing the boundaries of the one who came before. In Dewi Lestari's wildly popular first novel, "Supernova," the main characters include a gay couple and a prostitute. Djenar Maesa Ayu published a book of prize-winning short stories, including one entitled "Nursing From Daddy," in which she expresses a young woman's rejection of the traditional place of women in society through the metaphor of her suckling her father's penis instead of her mother's breast. And Dinar Rahayu, who wears the traditional Muslim hijab scarf in public, wrote about sadomasochism and transsexuality in her first book, "Ode to Leopold von

Sacher Masoch." Soon after it was published, she resigned her position as a chemistry teacher at a progressive, privately run Muslim high school. But like most of her peers, she made it onto Indonesia's top-10 best-seller lists. <+>

Some believe the sastra wangi writers are merely bringing to light the country's natural lustiness. "We Indonesians are a raunchy lot," says Julia Suryakusmana, academic, writer, publisher and self-proclaimed feminist. "We've got our own traditional culture that is very sexual. It's just that there is a schizophrenia between historical reality and what is called 'Eastern' values." That schizophrenia reached new heights under Suharto's long rule, from 1966 to 1998. After allowing an initial period of openness, in the early 1970s Suharto cracked down hard on all forms of critical and creative thinking. "For a period of about 25 years there was a lost generation in terms of Indonesian literature, when writers wrote more and more obliquely," says John McGlynn, director of publications at the Lontar Foundation, a nonprofit organization that translates Indonesian literature into English. "The refreshing thing--not just about the women writers but the whole generation of new writers--is they are reclaiming their voice."

"So far, that voice is in no danger of being silenced. Indonesia's Muslim leaders, who have been waging strict campaigns against pornography and suggestive dance shows on TV, have left the sastra wangi set alone. That may have less to do with the message than the medium; since most Indonesians don't read, literature is not deemed as dangerous as other media. "The religious establishment don't pay attention to art and literature because the impact of literature is limited," says Nirwan Derwanto, former editor of the respected journal Kalam. "One of the greatest things about the sastra wangi movement is, it is bringing people to literature." The hordes of women clamoring for Utami to sign copies of "Sex, Sketches and Stories" is clear proof of that.

A. Junaidi and Suryakusuma wrote in The Jakarta Post that sastra wangi writers have several things in common. The works tend to be launched in cafes and bookstores, with celebrities and reporters invited. The writers themselves are younger women, generally entering the industry around the age of 30, and often physically attractive. The works usually deal openly with sexuality, traditionally a taboo subject in Indonesian women's literature. This includes homosexuality. Suryakusuma notes that the traditional patriarchal view of sex, with the man as the subject and woman as the object, is reversed in these works, with women aggressively seeking and enjoying sex. The diction can be explicit, with terms such as 'penis' and 'vagina' being common. The diction and subject matter are often "shocking". Although works from a female perspective have been common in Indonesian literature, with works by Nh. Dini from the 1970s including references to sexuality, they were generally within the realm of social mores; the sastra wangi movement tends to go against these mores.

Indonesia's Twelve-Year-Old Novelist

In 2011, Deanna Ramsay wrote in the Jakarta Post, "A new addition to Indonesia's cohort of novelists has just emerged. Her name is Raisa Affandi, and she is just 11 years old. Raisa's first novel was published a little over a week ago. Titled Mimi Bo and the Missing Diary, the exuberant and inventive work is set in a sometimes dreamlike fantasyland. One part Harry Potter for its school setting amidst student intrigue, one part Charlie and the Chocolate Factory for its obsession with sweets and one part surrealist illusion a la the Beatles' "Lucy in the Sky with Diamonds", Mimi Bo and the Missing Diary at 195 pages is a remarkable achievement for someone so young. And, the novel was written in English.

"After spending some time with Raisa it is clear she is passionate about reading and writing, her room filled with books and remnants of her own compositions. When asked what had motivated her to embark upon writing a novel, Raisa said she was inspired by her younger sister Kyla. Raisa started writing Mimi Bo and the Missing Diary in 2008 right after Kyla was born and based the main character, Mimi Bo, on her beloved sister. Mimi Bo in the novel is a precocious child with a mind advanced well beyond her 3 months. As Raisa herself describes the work, "I just wanted to make a book about babies because I knew the pictures would be cute because babies are cute."

"But, the work is not just about babies; it is about children with an awareness of the world around them that is much deeper than the adults in the story imagine. For example, the babies cleverly use crying as a tactic to achieve other ends. When asked about the process of novel writing, which took her about a year, Raisa said, "At first I had no idea what the story was going to be about except there were these babies who were special at this special school. Then I just started adding more ideas and more ideas until the end."

"The book, adorned with vibrant watercolor drawings, is set at a school that is a virtual paradise for infants (and adults for that matter), featuring storks as public transportation, a rainbow club that meets during storms, an array of decadent sweet things to eat and a baby disco. There is also a mystery involving, as the title connotes, a missing diary, together with lively descriptions of sites borne out of a child's vivid imagination: healthy food that tastes likes strawberry ice cream, a door that leads to the tops of pillowy clouds and chocolate fountains and lemonade swimming pools.

"Raisa's parents said at first they were not even aware that she was writing a book until one day they saw her busily, and happily, typing away on the computer and asked her what she was doing. Now, Raisa says she imagines her initial work as part of a series, each book set in the following month of the school year. She has almost completed book two, which takes a somewhat different turn, featuring "a monster at the school [that] turns out to be a good person", secret agents and various sleuthing activities. She also invented a baby language for her book, Baahian, citing again her little sister's inspiration. Clearly, Raisa's interest lies in language; she is fluent in both English and Indonesian.

"Raisa spent four of her formative years living in Cambridge, England, while her father worked on his PhD and her mother an M.A., and English is essentially her first language. Currently living in Jakarta and attending an international school with instruction in both Indonesian and English, Raisa still prefers to read English-language books, saying she especially enjoys reading the Harry Potter series, The Necromancer and horror stories or "anything creepy".

Her parents also say that she will even pick up their books and peruse them, whether a text on economics or a work on probability theory.

History and Culture of Bali

The history of Bali goes back thousands of years. Sembiran, in northern Bali, is believed to have been home to Ice Age inhabitants, evidenced by the discovery of stone axes and other tools. Further archaeological discoveries such as sophisticated stone tools, agricultural techniques and basic pottery at Cekik in West Bali, are evidence of a settlement whose burial sites of around 100 people are believed to be from the Neolithic to the Bronze Age. Massive drums of the Bronze Age, together with their stone moulds, have been found throughout the Indonesian islands. The most famous and largest drum in Southeast Asia, the Moon of Pejeng - nearly two metres wide - is now on view in a temple in east Ubud, Central Bali. In the Bali

Museum in Denpasar and Purbakala Museum in Pejeng, there are collections of carved stone sarcophagi from a sophisticated civilisation.

Bali's earliest written records, prasasti, or metal inscriptions, from the 9th century AD, show a significant Buddhist and Hindu influence. This is especially true of the statues, bronzes and rock-cut caves around Mount Kawi and Gajah Cave. Balinese society was quite sophisticated by 900 AD. In the Pura Korah Tegipan in the Batur area, the marriage portrait of the Balinese King Udayana to East Java Princess Mahendratta is captured in a stone carving. Their son, Erlangga, succeeded to the throne of the Javanese Kingdom and brought Java and Bali together until his death in 1049. At that time, rice was already being grown under the complex irrigation system known as *subak,* and there were precursors of the religious and cultural traditions that can be seen in the region today.

Erlangga is reputed to be responsible for the spread of the Hindu influence into Bali from Java. He became one of Java's greatest kings, taking back the kingdom lost by his uncle. His mother had moved to Bali and remarried shortly after his birth, so when he gained the throne there was an immediate link between Java and Bali. The rock-cut memorials seen at Gunung Kawi (Mt. Kawi) near Tampaksiring are a clear architectural link between Bali and 11th-century Java.

After Erlangga's death, Bali retained its semi-independent status until Kertanagara became king of the Singasari dynasty in Java, and conquered Bali in 1284 - but after only eight years his kingdom collapsed. With Java in turmoil, Bali regained its autonomy and the Pejeng dynasty, centred near modern-day Ubud, rose to great power. In 1343 Gajah Mada, the legendary chief minister of the Majapahit dynasty, defeated the Pejeng king Dalem Bedaulu and brought Bali back under Javanese influence. This resulted in massive changes in Balinese society, including the introduction of the caste system.

Tribal Balinese who did not like the changes fled to isolated and remote mountainous areas. Their descendants are today known as Bali Aga or Bali Mula, meaning "original Balinese". They still live apart in villages like Tenganan near Dasa Temple, and Trunyan on the shores of Lake Batur; there they maintain their ancient laws and traditional ways.

Although Gajah Mada brought much of the Indonesian archipelago under Majapahit control, Bali was the furthest extent of its power. The capital moved to Gelgel, near modern-day Semarapura (formerly Klungkung), around the late 14th century, and for the next two centuries this was the base for the King of Bali, the Dewa Agung. The Majapahit kingdom collapsed into disputing sultanates. However, the Gelgel dynasty in Bali, under Dalem Batur Enggong, extended its power eastwards to the neighbouring island of Lombok and crossed the strait to Java on its west side.

When Majapahit in East Java fell in 1515, the many small Islamic kingdoms on the island merged into the Islamic Mataram empire. Majapahit's most dedicated Hindu priests, craftsmen, soldiers, nobles and artists fled east to Bali, and flooded the island with Javanese culture and Hindu practices. The refugees included the priest Nirartha, who is credited with introducing many of the complexities of Balinese religion to the island. Considering the huge influence and power of Islam at the time, one can only wonder why and how Bali still remained strongly Hindu.

Batu Renggong, also known as Dewa Agung, meaning "great god", became king in 1550, and this title became hereditary through the succeeding generations of the Kingdom of Gelgel, and later Klungkung, until the 20th century. Bali's decline began when Batu Renggong's grandson, Di Made Bekung, lost Blambangan, Lombok and Sumbawa. DI Made Bekung's chief minister, Gusti

Agung Maruti, eventually rebelled and reigned from 1650 until 1686, when he in turn was killed by DI Made Bekung's son, Dewa Agung Jambe, who then moved the court to Klungkung, and named his new palace the Semarapura: Abode of the God of Love.

The first Europeans - Dutch sailors - were seen in Bali in 1597. In 1602 a group of Dutch merchants and independent trading companies, impatient with the monopoly the Portuguese had established over the spice trade with East Asia at the end of the 15th century and keeping the British imperial merchants in check, founded the Vereenigde Landsche Ge-Oktroyeerde Oostindische Compagnie, the VOC, better known as the Dutch East India Company. The executive directorate of the VOC was called the Heeren Sewentien or the "Lords Seventeen".

The VOC was granted a government charter, which effectively guaranteed it a spice trade monopoly in East Asia. However, this government charter secured the VOC more than a trade monopoly: it gave the VOC the power to colonise whichever territory it desired, enslaving the indigenous people according to market requirements and VOC political imperatives. This meant that the VOC did not merely become involved in trade wars with European and Asian powers from its headquarters in Batavia, but waged full-scale warfare on indigenous people in those countries that would not cooperate with its demands for spices such as cloves, nutmeg and pepper, or who resisted the cash-crop economy that the VOC was forcing onto them by establishing plantations. A prime example is the island of Banda in the Indonesian Archipelago. The VOC simply killed off the Bandanese, appropriated the island, and cultivated nutmeg as a monoculture, using slave labour from neighbouring countries.

The VOC monopoly of the spice trade meant that it set the prices of commodities, their production and availability. In addition the VOC developed the world's first stock market in Amsterdam, with durable assets and controlled investment schemes. As a result, a number of trading stations were built across East Asia. In 1652 Jan van Riebeeck had "taken over" the Cape of Good Hope and established a replenishment station, using political prisoners brought from Batavia and other Asian islands. In terms of trade and commerce, Holland reached the height of its power in this period.

In 1710 the capital of the Gelgel kingdom of Bali shifted to Klungkung (now Semarapura), but local discontent was growing, lesser rulers were breaking away from Gelgel domination and the Dutch began to move in, using the old policy of divide and conquer. In 1846 the Dutch used Balinese salvage claims over shipwrecks as the pretext to land military forces in northern Bali. In 1894 the Dutch chose to support the Sasaks of Lombok, which had been invaded by the Balinese. After a rebellion against their Balinese Rajah in bloody battles, the Balinese were defeated in Lombok, and northern Bali came firmly under Dutch control.

The Dutch could not gain control over South Bali for some years, but later "salvaging disputes" gave them the excuse they needed to move in. A Chinese ship was wrecked off Sanur in 1904 and ransacked by the Balinese. The Dutch demanded that the rajah of Badung pay 3000 silver dollars in damages – this was refused. In 1906 Dutch warships appeared at Sanur and started a naval bombardment of Denpasar and then commenced their final assault. Their forces landed and, despite Balinese opposition, marched to the outskirts of Denpasar.

The three rajahs of Badung (southern Bali) realised that they were outnumbered and outgunned, and that defeat was inevitable. Surrender and exile, however, was the worst imaginable outcome, so they decided to take the honourable path of a suicidal *puputan* – a fight to the death. Row after row of the Balinese nobility and their servants marched forward to their deaths. In all, nearly 4000 Balinese died in the *puputan*. Later, the Dutch marched towards Tabanan and took the rajah of Tabanan prisoner, but he committed suicide rather than face the disgrace of exile.

The kingdoms of Karangasem and Gianyar had already capitulated to the Dutch and were allowed to retain some powers, but other kingdoms were defeated and the rulers exiled. Finally, the rajah of Klungkung followed the lead of Badung and once more the Dutch faced a *puputan*. With this last obstacle disposed of, all of Bali was under Dutch control and became part of the Dutch East Indies. Dutch rule over Bali was short-lived, however, as Indonesia fell to the Japanese in WWII.

Independence

When Japan was defeated and had to leave the Dutch East Indies, British Colonel Laurens van der Post was made Allied Commander of the country. It was quite an irony that an English South African with a Dutch father and German mother had to tell the Dutch troops landing back in "their" Indies that they were no longer welcome. He saw the events which brought about Indonesian political change. On 17 August 1945, the Indonesian leader Soekarno proclaimed the nation's independence. In a virtual repeat of the *puputan,* nearly half a century earlier, a Balinese resistance group was wiped out by Dutch troops in the Battle of Marga, on 20 November 1946. Bali's Ngurah Rai Airport is named after the group's leader and his 96 troops. It was not until 1949 that the Dutch finally recognised Indonesia's independence.

A massive eruption of Gunung Agung in 1963 killed thousands, devastated vast areas of the island and forced many Balinese to accept transmigration to other parts of Indonesia. Two years later, in the wake of an attempted communist coup, Bali became the scene of some of the bloodiest anti-communist killings in Indonesia.

The tourism boom, which started in the early 1970s, has brought many changes, and has helped pay for improvements in roads, telecommunications, education and health. Bali's unique culture has proved remarkably resilient to tourism's influence. Beginning in the 1990s there has been vocal public opposition to some controversial developments, which indicates that

Balinese people will play a more active role in the future of their island.

Bali, like most places, has also been affected by global politics. In October 2002, two simultaneous bomb explosions in Kuta – targeting an area frequented by tourists – injured or killed more than 500 people. The island's vital tourist industry was dealt a severe blow. It had mostly recovered by 2005, when in October of that year more bombs went off, albeit with less loss of life. Still, the bombs caused an immediate sharp drop in tourism and have forced the Balinese to yet again ponder their role in the world's greater geopolitics. Fortunately, memories have faded a bit, and tourism has returned to Bali in a big way.

Bali Travel Guide

Things to Do in Bali

So were you wondering if there's anything to do on an island covered in rice paddies and tropical jungle? Or did you just want to sit in the sun and drink beer? Well, some people do. Then the rest of us get out and experience the real Bali.

If you like the outdoors, there is certainly no shortage of activities on Bali. For divers we have over 952 species of sea life and 393 coral species. You can scuba-dive or snorkel all around Bali or its baby islands Nusa Lembongan and Nusa Penida. Surfers do not need to be told that Bali has some of the most awesome waves in the world. Just ask the ASP why they are having

Phase 5 of their World Championships here. In the centre of the island one can go white-water rafting, canyoning, motor- or pedal bike riding, or offroading in various types of vehicles.Families will love Bali Zoo or Safari Park, Taro Elephant Park, Bali Bird Park and more. Botanists, come and see the spectacular collections of orchids and 111 other indigenous plants. Twitchers, come catch some birds in your binocs. Want to go riding? Horse or elephant?Sailors will have a grand time, either at the Royal Bali Yacht Club, or on a schooner bound for the islands east of here. Of course you can also fly there - by charter seaplane or helicopter. Sky's the limit.

Yeh Gangga Offroad - Bali

Come see the real Balinese countryside where larger vehicles can't go; on one of the ATV's in the Gangga Squad. Scoot along empty beaches, look down from seaside cliffs on stunning beaches, view a renowned Temple built on a rock in the sea, meander through

rice fields amnd visit sleepy villages as the cocks crow.
Ride solo or with co-pilot.

Single or tandem riders: 2 hours $85 or $130.
Pick-up and drop-off in a/c vehicles, light refreshments, cool drinks.
You bring: Change of clothes, shorts or longs, shoes, sunscreen, camera, towel - you could get dirty!
Experienced guides go with you. Insurance cover.

Blanco Renaissance Museum - Bali

The Blanco Renaissance Museum was once the home of world famous Antonio Blanco, the most famous foreign artist ever to lay down roots in Bali. He has created and sold works to Mick Jagger, Ingrid Bergman and Michael Jackson and is known for his eccentric and unique style. He married a Balinese dancer and raised his children in their home on top of a mountain which overlooks the Campuan River. Since Blanco's death in 1999, the building and his studio have been open to the public as a museum, realising a personal dream of the artist.

Antonio Blanco was born to Spanish parents who settled in the Philippines in 1911. He moved to Bali penniless, befriended the King and became the confidant of many powerful folks in Indonesia. His museum displays most of his paintings and artwork that involved baroque pornography, mostly women with exposed breasts. It has a wonderful garden patio that also has a corner for petting bird station.

Mario Blanco, Antonio's son, has since kept up the artistic tradition and helps run the grounds, as well as creating his own paintings. His style is a fusion of Balinese and European - his 'naturalistic, impressionist' oil paintings are unique and mesmerising.

The collection of Antonio Blanco's work is sensual, eccentric and erotic - whether you're an avid art-lover or new to the scene, you will be entertained. And with The Bridges restaurant next door, you can make a day of it.

Opening times: 09.00 - 17.00
Admission: tourists: Rp. 50,000

Bali Orchid Garden - Bali

Within this relaxing tropical garden, in a peaceful environment along the green belt of Sanur, we grow many different tropical plants from Cordylines, Bromeliads, Heliconia, Aroids, Pitcher plants (nepenthes) and many more from Indonesia and abroad. Orchids range from showy cattleya and vanda hybrids to a large range of Indonesian species. Our exquisite orchids bloom throughout the year.

Bali Orchid Garden was founded and developed by experienced orchid growers David and Dorothy Dowd. It is Bali's original Orchid Garden developed specially for overseas and local tourists, complementing the government botanical garden, and is situated within easy reach of the many tourist hotels in South Bali.

Bali Orchid Garden offers services such as landscaping, private and group tours and hosting of special functions like wedding photography. The souvenir shop is well stocked with a wide variety of products for sale.

Friendly Balinese staff are available to escort clients and explain the wide variety of tropical plants and help you discover many orchid treasures while touring the garden, or assist with your purchase of a memento from the shop. Flower boxes can be ordered to take overseas. Floral arrangements and plants are also available for local use.

Bali Orchid Garden is committed to preserving the orchid species of Indonesia. A partnership has been formed with Bogor Botanical Garden to propagate these indigenous species and ensure they will be available for future generations of orchid enthusiasts to enjoy. A proportion of each sale is used to promote the program of propagation and conservation of local varieties.

The garden's well stocked souvenir shop offers diverse products including flasks of orchid plants. Boxes of tropical flowers including Heliconia, Anthuriums and Orchids purchased to take home, have full export clearance papers provided and can be delivered to your hotel. Flower arrangements and bouquets of flowers are prepared for special occasions.

We offer hotel room decorations, flowers for weddings and special occasions, wholesale and retail cut flowers, flasks of orchid seedlings, species and hybrids for local and export sale, special group and school tours of Gardens.

The Chillhouse - Bali

The Chillhouse is a traditional retreat situated in Canggu amongst the rice fields on the southern shores of Bali, offering guest's quality accommodation and delicious organic meals, along with surf guiding, massage treatments, yoga sessions, and a wide range of fitness as well as cultural activities.

The retreat features full board, The Gerry Lopez Treetop Loft, six luxurious double bungalows with private gardens, single and double rooms, a spacious pool, unlimited wi-fi internet and Canggu Club membership.

The Chillhouse is a place where you can indulge in an unforgettable surfing holiday, filled with endless waves and maximum comfort. The emphasis of course is on surfing but not just about chasing waves. With various packages available, it is our desire to make you and your family feel at home.

Eka Karya Botanic Garden - Bali

The Garden is situated near the mountain tourist resorts of Bedugul and Candikuning, on the east slope of Bukit Tapak Hill, at an elevation of 1,250 to 1,400m and is beside Batukau Nature Reserve (15,390 ha). The Eka Kaya Garden is a branch of Kebun Raya Bogor on Java.

Daytime temperature is about 17-25C, falling to 10 -15 C at night with humidity 70-90%. The cool climate, with annual rainfall 3,000mm, clean air and beautiful scenery in its mountainous setting, with adjacent forests, the lake and the attractive landscape all blending harmoniously, make this garden a popular spot away from the heat in the south of the island. It provides a place where you can relax in peaceful surroundings while learning about the use of plants in the daily lives of Balinese people as well as many interesting tropical rainforest plants and birdlife.

Eka Karya Garden is unique in Bali as a centre for botanical research, education and recreation, and is a forerunner in conserving Indonesia's flora. Students use the plant collection for extra-curricular study. In order to fulfil this task, Eka Karya Garden, conducts field exploration and surveys, and has been equipped with an herbarium, seed collection, and nursery, as well as the living collections of trees, ferns, orchids, cacti and other plants of scientific, economic, cultural and aesthetic value.

Visitors arriving at the Eka Karya Botanic Garden, Bali, will immediately notice the special Balinese architecture, which is both sturdy and beautiful. The distinctive carved split candi bentar at the main entrance is typical of those usually found in temples or important buildings in Bali.

The Garden has an extensive Gymnosperm (non-flowering plants) collection, imported from many regions of the world, including The Netherlands, Australia, Japan, China, Africa, North and South America. The collection of woody plants totals 656 species from 141 families, some of which are indigenous to the gardens, in particular, the native Cemara Pandak (Podocarpus javanicus).

The social fabric of Balinese life cannot be separated from traditional ceremony and religious activity. The raw materials of many well-known plants play an important part in sacred ceremonies. Because of their importance, Eka Karya Garden began, in 1991, to make inventories, collections and plantings of species used for traditional ceremonies. To date, the collection consists of 454 specimens from 117 species.

Within the gardens is a traditional Balinese house, called the Ethnobotany Building as it contains the Garden's collection of ethnobotanical artifacts. Traditional Balinese houses are a collection of smaller houses each with a particular function which are enclosed within or just outside of a perimeter wall.

More than 2000 species of plants are preserved at Bali Botanic Garden, representing plants from eastern Indonesia: Bali, Nusa Tenggara, Sulawesi, Maluku and Papua. New plants are acquired from commercial nurseries, arboreta, botanic gardens, plant breeding programmes and collecting expeditions. Because of its unique site incorporating landscape gardens with native habitat, the Garden is able to assimilate terrestrial and aquatic plants found in similar habitats.

Seeds and plants are accepted only if their provenance is known and documented and only if they have been collected and imported legally. Plants that have the potential for invasiveness, genetic pollution or introducing pests or diseases are carefully screened. In

Indonesia there are approximately 4000 species of orchid, about half of which occur in Papua. Very little is known about the diversity of orchids. The Bali Botanic Garden has prioritised collecting wild Indonesian orchid species, mainly from the mountain forests of Bali, Java, Nusa Tenggara, Sulawesi and Papua.

The Begonia collections are planted in a beautiful park and in a special Begonia house. The park design is based on a natural concept that mimics the natural habitat of begonias in general. More than 200 species of begonias are collected and propagation has reached thousand of plants so it is appropriate that Bali Botanic Garden has become the centre of Begonia conservation in Indonesia.

The cactus collection is located in a big glasshouse near the office. Many species have beautiful and colourful flowers. Taman Usada (Usada garden) has recently been established in the nursery. This garden, which covers 1600 m2, was built in mid-2005 as implementation of the conservation effort of Bali

Botanic Garden for Balinese medicinal plants. The Aquatic plant collections are arranged in six stair ponds and decorated with stones and pots.

S2S CrossFit - Bali

The mission is to introduce this elite training programme to the island and to bring people together as a tight-knit community. S2S CrossFit is in a tranquil setting next to a paddy field and up the road from the beach. WODs (workout of the day) in multiple places - the box, the soccer field next door and Brawa Beach.

Every day, athletes get a new WOD which consists of constantly varied functional movements performed in high intensity, varying from Olympics weightlifting, gymnastics to metabolic conditioning (cardio). All workouts are scaled to your ability. Find your threshold and ensure you continuously perform at maximum intensity. Classes are one hour, covering warm-up, warm-down, a mix of strength and metcon (metabolic conditioning).

Recommend you join initial CrossFit 2-week Elements programme before joining the normal class. Elements sessions will teach the fundamental movements of CrossFit and its methodology incl. health and nutrition.

Celebrity Fitness - Bali

Celebrity Fitness is the first international fitness chain to open on Bali. Members and fans across Indonesia, Malaysia and Singapore who can now stay fit even while on holiday.

Celebrity Clubs offer 5 DAYS FREE PREMIER ACCESS trials.

The different membership tiers on offer at Celebrity Fitness are:

One club - unlimited access to all facilities and classes at one named Celebrity Fitness club.

Premier - unlimited access to all facilities and classes at all Jakarta to all Kuala Lumpur clubs

VIP - unlimited access to all facilities and classes to all Celebrity Fitness clubs in all countries, dedicated VIP suites at changing rooms in selected club, exclusive merchandise and offers

Family - save as much as 75% on your monthly payment when you join as a family.

Corporate - preferential rates for companies and their employees.

Student - for those looking for an early start to their fitness journey.

Ubud Fitness Center - Bali

Ubud's only fully-equipped, air-conditioned gym with complete cardio and weight equipment can be found at Jln. Jero Gadung, just 500 meters up from Jl. Raya, where friendly and experienced personal trainers who can help you reach all of your fitness targets.

Memberships to suit every need, with daily, weekly, monthly and yearly rates. The entire team is dedicated to making your fitness experience an exceptional one.

Working with a personal trainer is one of the fastest, most successful ways to improve your health and fitness. No longer the domain of the wealthy and famous, personal trainers are now employed by people from all walks of life who want to get the most out of their exercise.

Ubud Fitness Centre has its own squash court, aerobics/boxing room, hot showers, towels. Free Wi-Fi to members and guests. Fresh smoothies and juices at the Terrace Cafe.

Sunrise School of Surfing - Bali

Come shop, eat, play, hangout and listen to cool bands! We are also celebrating the grand opening of the MTC Centre for children with physical disabilities!

Students at Bali Sunrise School are invited to reflect, imagine, communicate, create, write about, artistically express and play with values. In the process, personal, social and emotional skills develop.

Our purpose is to encourage confidence, compassion, awareness, responsibility and creativity in each student, by providing an integrated educational atmosphere with a strong emphasis on environmental sustainability and creative arts.

To these ends, Sunrise School in #Bali endeavours to:
Support students to meet academic, social and emotional challenges with openness, enthusiasm and a willingness to solve problems.
Encourage students to think globally, act locally and feel totally.
Foster an atmosphere of cooperation, with respect for individual differences in the context of community values.
Maintain a balance between freedom and structure in the context of everyday experiences.
Appreciate the unique contributions to society made by people from all economic, religious, racial and social backgrounds, as well as from those of different physical ability
Provide a holistic learning environment based on a simple principle:

Bali Zoo - Bali

Bali Zoo is home to more than 350 creatures in 22 acres of lush vegetation, with gently rolling terrain, simulating the animals' natural habitat. Situated in the cultural heart of Bali, the zoo is only a ten minute drive from Ubud and about forty five minutes from the tourist areas of Kuta, Tuban, Legian and Seminyak. The sandy white beaches of Sanur are a twenty minute drive away. Nearby you can grab a bargain at the Sukawati market, or head into Ubud to visit some exquisite galleries and boutiques. Take a drive and discover hidden temples, lush green rice terraces, and the world famous smiles of the locals.

Come and spend a day and experience the beauty of Bali Zoo surroundings, learn about awesome animals, and hopefully create memories that you will cherish for a long time. Bali's only zoo, is a 'Nature's Education Centre'. Friendly staff are eager to show you around, talk to you about animals, how to make their lives more comfortable, and what YOU can do if you would like to help. Bali Zoo staff have a 'hands on' approach to conservation education, and love to share ideas with you.

Visitors are welcomed by the lion family, the warm song of the Siamangs, a lazy gigantic crocodile, and the biggest lizard in the world, the Komodo Dragon! Plus Sumatran elephant, Sumatran tiger, orangutan, sun bear, kangaroos, camels, deer and Binturong; reptiles like iguanas, pythons, green snakes; birds like cassowaries, peacocks, and Bali Starlings and many more animals.

Daily program includes feeding of the lions, crocodiles and tigers, and if it's cute and cuddly that you're after - why not head down to the petting area and snuggle with a baby monkey? All of the inhabitants are fully cared for by the resident veterinarian, and the Zoo is a bird flu free environment.

Bali Bird Park - Bali

Bali Bird Park is located in Singapadu, near Celuk. Home to 250 different species of birds, it is the biggest and the best bird park in all of Bali. Though it features a fantastic collection of Indonesian birds, it also boasts some amazing species from Africa and South America. In its two hectares of botanical gardens, the park is a sanctuary for nearly 1000 individual birds and an amazing display of flora: more than 2000 tropical plants, including 50 varieties of palms alone. It's no surprise that it attracts swarms of gorgeous butterflies.

The park is divided into sections representing and recreating various Indonesian habitats, with their native birds and plants. You'll see endangered bird species of birds from Bali such as the Bali Starling, the fantastic Java hawk, serpent eagles, parrots, flamingos, storks, pelicans, green peafowl, Asian pied hornbills, Javan kingfishers and exotic birds from Papua. In the East Indonesia section you can meet not just birds, but the extraordinary Komodo Dragon as well - a direct descendant of the dinosaurs, rarely seen in captivity.

The Park's approach to displaying rare and tropical birds has shifted from traditional exhibits to showcasing mixed species in their natural habitats. The complex incorporates breeding, research and veterinary facilities and has a high success rate in the reproduction of exotic birds.

There are many native Indonesian, Australian and South American species of parrots bred in the park. Look for the White Cockatoo from the Molucca Islands, known to live up to 80 years. In recent times their numbers in the wild have significantly decreased due to habitat loss and illegal trapping. Palm Cockatoos are known for the 20 or more different kinds of vocalisations they make, including a 'hello' call that is surprisingly human-like. Listen too for the very distinctive, loud call of the endangered Bali Starling.

The park and restaurant are open from 09.00 until 17:30 daily.

Amed Dive Centre - Bali

Amed Dive Centre in East Bali works in close cooperation with Hotel Uyah Amed and Spa Resort and offers fun dives, snorkelling and diving and accommodation packages.

Amed Dive Center offers Introductory Dives, Scuba Diving, PADI and SSI Open Water Dive Courses, PADI

Advanced Open Water Dive Courses, SSI Advanced Adventure Dive Courses, Rescue Diver Course, Emergency First Response and Fun Diving at Bali's best Dive Sites.

'Make Bubbles Not Troubles' is the motto of Amed Dive Centre.

Introductory Dive Package:
1 night accommodation & 2 intro dives (1 day, 2 dives)
1 person, single occupation - € 87,- / € 73,-
2 persons, double occupation - € 109,- / € 92,-

Amed Dive Center offers relaxed and enjoyable water sport, optimum safety, focus on sustainable development, special diving courses and trips focusing on environmental issues, staff trained in safety, health and environmental matters.

Taman Nusa Cultural Park - Bali

Taman Nusa Cultural Centre contains a comprehensive physical history of Indonesia's many tribal groups in an attractive setting in the hills of Bali near Gianyar.

Within the 15 hectare grounds, visitors are taken through the development of the islands, starting with: Prehistoric Era, Bronze Age, Kingdom Age.

It then continues to Early Indonesia, Indonesian Independence, Present Day Indonesia and Future Indonesia.

Besides a Living Museum with Wayang, Batik, weaving and embroidery, a Static Museum and Library, there is a miniature stone replica of Borrobudur Temple, handmade in Java and transported on 80 trucks to the site.

The same applies to many of the dwellings, purchased from island folk and re-erected on the site. Many are 100's of years old. The view of the indigenous forest in the gorge and up the other side is an added bonus while enjoying lunch in the restaurant.

Dojo Aora Judo - Bali

Dojo Aora was formed in 2003 in conjunction with the Bali Judo Community declaration. Judo teacher Claude Thouvenel originates from Perpignan, France, where he studied athletics and to be a judo teacher. Claude now owns and manages the Dojo Aora Judo School in Seminyak.

The original Japanese judo was created in 1882 by Shingoro Kano, from jiu jitsu, a method of fighting in vogue in the 16th century. The fighting style was at the heart of Japanese feudalism and was practiced in the dojo, a room with Japanese tatamis mats or carpets.

Judo is a fun and friendly sport, an activity which will enrich the lives of children. It works for all children from the age of four. Judo helps children develop physically and mentally, to gain confidence and to build good relationships with others. Besides the skill of defending them elves, children learn - Sincerity - Respect - Modesty - Politeness - Honour - Courage - Self-control.

Bali Cycling Operator - Bali

Experienced in implementing cycling events, training and preparation of domestic bikes or sport bikes. Providing bicycles, escort cycling, biking locations, support car and all forms related to the sport of cycling. Bali Cycling Operator assists individuals, groups on race cycling, mountain bike touring, family cycling and triathlon training

Introduce your family to the natural beauty from Kintamani to Ubud, Bali on bicycles. The family cycling program is easy. High quality mountain bikes. Enjoy stunning views and a superb insight into Balinese culture and way of life.

Race bike program on roads for individuals or groups. The roads in Bali are comfortable for cycling training and sport holidays.

Adventure Cycling with Sobek - Bali

Discover hidden Bali along the paths and trails leading down from Pengotan village. Escape the tourist crowds and head for the cool atmosphere of Srubatu Valley on brand new mountain bikes, with all safety equipment provided.

Follow experienced guides on the route through rice paddy fields and traditional villages, past ancient temples and through rain forests and jungle. Stop at local villages to get the feel of the real Bali, in the countryside, where many things have not changed for centuries. 2.5 hour ride ends with a much-needed lunch in Ubud, in the mountains and jungle of Bali. Price: Adult US$79, children US$52. Pick-ups from Nusa Dua, Jimbaran, Kuta, Sanur, Ubud.

Pack your sunscreen, and maybe a change of clothes in case you encounter mud - it rains a lot in

Komune Resort & Beach Club - Bali
Night Surfing at Keramas

Come to the scene of last year's Oakley Pro Bali WCT and watch surfers doing it at night - night surfing! I saw the bright lights from Hai Tide Huts on Nusa Lembongan last year and asked the waitresses what they were. Of course, they were the lights on Pantai Keramas, where you, too, can watch the night surfing while staying over at the Komune Resort.

See the incredible show put on by fearless surfers, or join in the fun if you dare. Stay over and watch world-class waves in front of your villa, day and night. Watch the Keramas waves start as top to bottom barrels, with a lightening fast high performance end. That's why Oakley chose this venue for 1 of the 9 surfing contests in the Oakley International Contest last year.

Go out and try one yourself. There are local surfers to advise you.
Our pool is also spectacular and the outdoor dining is an adventure in itself.

Komune offers a few 'right on the beach' villas and several further back, all just 2 minutes to the surf. Villas are for daily rental or outright sale.

Surf Goddess Retreats - Bali

Come learn how to 'hang ten' in a fun and supportive environment with like-minded ladies. Surf Goddess Retreats are a great way to learn surfing and yoga. The 7 - 8 day programs include plenty of time out on the water with accredited surf instructors from the Rip Curl School of Surf, as well as tasty gourmet meals, super spa sessions to soothe aching muscles, restorative yoga classes and amazing trips around the island to learn more about Balinese culture and see the unique landscape that is #Bali.

Guests of Surf Goddess Retreats stay in a beautiful colonial villa, 'Barefoot Chic' exclusively for Surf Goddesses, set in lush tropical gardens just minutes from the beach at Seminyak, famous for its restaurants and night life. The rooms offer all modern amenities you would expect, including soft linens, iPod stereo docks, hair dryers and custom blended spa products. Each room also has large windows that look out over the garden and allow soft breezes to flow in.

Hours in a relaxing spa where you get to choose the treatments you desire - Time for Wellness and Transformation - Opportunities for Healing and Personal Growth - Experience a Surf, Yoga & Spa Holiday Fit For a Goddess!

Nightlife in Bali

Bali nightlife can range from sedate dining on a cruise boat to exclusive upmarket restaurants representing many nations - not least Indonesia, and Bali in particular. Many a renowned chef has started his career here, then come back to a top post.

Most important of all, the food here is always fresh, and service is always with a smile. If you are into music, there is the choice between thumping Rock or smoothe Jazz or Blues, with salsa and other dancing venues all over the island. You will find a spectacular variety of cocktail bars, Karaoke bars, roof-top bars, English and Irish pubs, Italian cafés and night clubs. Stage shows are spectacular, and many restaurants bring on their lithe and talented Balinese dancers to entertain guests. There are even a few cinemas, with English language movies on offer. For the really adventurous, there are night-time elephant rides or dining with the lions - well, there is a glass window between you!

Old Man's

Canggu's classic surf club hangout, Old Man's describes itself as a 'beachfront beer garden'. With its laid back easy comfort seating, this family friendly beach bar and cafe is the perfect hangout spot for all ages, come day or night.

The vibrant colours and artwork surrounding the large open breezy spaces were commissioned by artist Lucas Grogan, and give Old Man's its instantly recognisable fun flair.

With a menu offering a variety of both international and local comfort foods, Old Mans' entices you to enjoy a more relaxed pace of living. The infamous happy hour from 17:00-18:00 daily brings a refreshing crowd of locals, expats and travelers and live bands and Djs are regular evening highlights.

The energy cranks up a little more on Wednesday nights with the classic 'Dirty Ol' Wednesdays' complete with beer pong competitions, drinking games and a full on dance floor, where a younger party scene fills the space. Sunday evenings at Old Man's are also seeing a growing crowd with themed parties and all star Djs spinning through to midnight.

Contrasting the party scene and in keeping with Old Man's success as a venue for all ages, weekly Saturday markets offer a place for all the family to come and enjoy a relaxed day out by the beach and source some local crafts and goodies.

Cocoon Beach Club - Bali

Under the palm trees and frangipanis of beautiful Bali, lies one of the most luxurious venues on the Island's west coast, Cocoon Restaurant and Beach Club.

Inspired by the idyllic surroundings of the famous Bali beaches and combined with Mediterranean flair, Cocoon offers fine dining, pool side lounging, and a relaxed ambience. A multi-faceted venue, Cocoon provides its guests with a relaxed and informal style of wining and dining during the day, and then transforms itself into a luxurious fine dining venue in the evening. Long after the sun has gone down and desser ts devoured, Cocoon transforms again into a sophisticated bar / lounge offering the best in music, cocktails and a fashionably savvy crowd.

You will be mesmerized by the design and architecture of our amazing space. Glide through the main dining area, past the Miami inspired bar and you will ultimately reach the jewel in our crown, our poolside area. With Azure blue under-tones and soft opulent furnishings, there is no better place to relax and chill out poolside whilst watching the Indian Ocean lapping at the shore and sipping on fresh and exotic cocktails. You can also indulge in our pool side grazing menu, offering a large range of delectable delights. Catering for Brunch, Lunch and Dinner in over three distinct dining areas, Cocoon menu's deliver a truly international cuisine with dishes fusing the best of Asian and modern European flavours and produce, our experts in the kitchen have created culinary delights that will have your mouth watering before you even order.

Since its inception in July 2010, Cocoon has hosted some of the Island's hottest events. DJ's and musicians from around the world have graced our poolside entertainment area.

Weddings and private events are also catered for with Cocoons dedicated team of event and wedding planners to ensure every element of your wedding or event runs smoothly and is beautifully delivered.

No Mas Ubud

Your Island Sinkhole Awaits

No Más is Ubud's long awaited new local bar, where Eagles of Death Metal is loud on Thursday, Jameson & Captain Morgans are tossed around on Fridays, and cougars prance around on Saturdays. Rotating Bands and DJ Gigs are a regular fixture while tunes from the likes of Bowie, Depeche Mode and Black Keys will be the norm throughout.

Drinks are crafted by throwing caution to the wind using the finest house pours, mixed by trainee bartenders and served by inexperienced wait-staff. The food never detracts from the serious business of shooting the shit, throwing back picklebacks, "going within, discussing failed marriages and bad app ideas, aptly name No Más (No More), the squad take no responsibility in bad decision-making up there.'

Because there's no shame in mediocrity. Live and let Live

40 Thieves

One of Seminyak's hippest new bars and drinking spots, 40 Thieves is the brainchild of international award-winning mixologist Shah Dillon. With a trendy New York style speakeasy concept and industrial themed décor to match, the focus on custom cocktails and artisanal craft spirits is key to the experience. Located on the upper floor above Mad Ronin ramen eatery, 40 Thieves has become a popular destination for Seminyak party-goers, offering a more laid-back and easy going alternative to the bigger and less personal nightclubs and discos on the Petitenget nightlife circuit.

La Favela - Bali

Famous for the coolest parties in Seminyak, La Favela is definitely one of the best must-go hotspots in Bali!

Some say it's 'vintage designed'. Others say Johnny Depp had a hand in it, as well as Salvador Dali (in spirit). La Favela is not only the funkiest or the most eclectic and spacious bar-restaurant in Bali, it is an amazing place to be. It has a soul!

It brings back memories and it is a statement on how old walls and objects can be given life without losing shape, form and originality. The exquisite decor was inspired by the Brazilian 'favelas'. Be sure to take your camera!

Red Carpet Champagne Bar - Bali

Without a doubt, Red Carpet Champagne Bar is among the favourite drinking and social hangouts of local expats and returning visitors to Bali.

Situated in the heart of Seminyak on Jalan Laksmana, a steady flow of buzzing of word-of-mouth has kept the Red Carpet thriving since opening - and turned it into a Seminyak icon. The joint is cozy and intimate, with a splash of sexiness. As can be expected of a 'champagne bar,' there is an exclusive feel - yet the atmosphere remains light, playful and fun.

Red Carpet Bar can proudly claim to have Indonesia's largest champagne collection, with well over a hundred bottles on the menu. Ranging from one million rupiah for Moët by the glass, all the way up to a $2200 bottle of 2002 Cristal - they are sure to have in stock both the most popular brands to surprise even the most diserning connoisseurs.

Rock Bar - Bali

The whole Ayana resort runs a mile along the coastline, but the Rock bar is the epitome of luxury below the cliffs. Ayana is huge and has a hotel with 290 rooms as well as a number of luxury private villas for guests to retreat to. The CNN and The New York Times have both described the bar as one of the best in the entire world, and in 2011 it was voted the best venue to watch the sunset in Indonesia. Surely guests should not require any more encouragement than that.

The bar has a 360 degree vista across cliffs, coral reef and ocean and guests are treated to the sound of the waves and the sun setting beyond the horizon every night. The bar was designed by a Japanese artist, meaning clean lines and minimalism are the focus of its vibrancy. The wooden decking and tables that surround the central bar all allow guests to experience the elegance and natural beauty at the Ayana resort but still feel intimate. At sunset the bar can be really busy and there may be queues so get in early or buy VIP passes to avoid disappointment. The dress code is formal after dark.

Once the sun has set, get ready to party, with a wide selection of cocktails designed by the 'bar consultant' Bonnefoi. These cocktails are not your usual tipple, they use imported liquors blended with local herbs and fruits to enliven the senses and the party spirit. There is also entertainment with live bands, DJ's and regular appearances from guest sets with Andy Caldwell and DJ Bruno from the clubs of Ibiza.

Pretty Poison

Hipster's Paradise. Pretty Poison's alternative skate-concept-bar offers a fresh new edge to Canggu's growing nightlife scene. Hang out in the back yard by the 'Dog Bowl', an 80s California style deep bowl skate pool with a bucket of cold beers and some light bites. Weekly skate jams, live music, resident DJs, indie movie screenings, tattoos and skate boards attract a refreshing mix of locals and expats to the Gu's hottest underground address.

UNIQUE Rooftop Bar Lounge & Restaurant - Bali

The new dinner menu and ladies' nights at the ultra-chic UNIQUE Rooftop Bar Lounge.

Monday and Thursday are Flirty Nights for ladies, with a complimentary first drink UNIQUE cocktail upon arrival from 6pm to catch the panoramic sunset views across the Uluwatu coastline - and a special price on this cocktail all night at just IDR 80,000++.

The 25-meter long rooftop pool offers all-day fun in the sun, while the new dinner menu entices UNIQUE's sunset crowd to extend their stay for Asian-inspired food such as Caramelized Angus Beef Cheek Skewers, Crispy Salted Pork Loin, Korean-spiced Chicken Wings, Whole Tail Scampi, Thai Red Duck Curry. Asian flavors are the perfect complement to heady cocktail concoctions like Rose Mary-Me with rum, lychee liqueur, fresh rosemary and lemongrass, or Spicy Colada - a twist on a Pina Colada with nutmeg and tabasco for some kick.

Minimum order 2 x UNIQUE Crush cocktails

Sky Garden - Bali

Nightclub, Cocktail Bar, and Lounge - Hours: Tuesday 5:00 pm - 4:00 am

Sky Garden is probably one of the best clubs in Bali. It is always full and happening. Actually, for many tourists, Bali nightlife equals spending the whole night in Sky Garden.

The official name of Sky Garden is '61 Legian', a huge entertainment complex with 7 different areas and Sky Garden is just one of them (the rooftop on top of the building). The others are:

ESC Urban Food Station: A food court opened until 5am
Blarney Stone: An Irish Pub with sports, live music, premium beer and pub food
Club Cyclone: The room with House Music
Brandy's Club: The room with RnB music
Heineken Beer Garden: Self-explanatory
VIP Gold Pass Lounge: For the wannabe VIP
The VIP Sky High Club: For the VVIP
George's Sports: Open 24/7 with sports, beer and food.
It can, however, get a bit rowdy and if you're a girl you have to watch that people don't attempt to take advantage of you. That being said, I went with a group of 4 girls almost every night of our stay and we always managed to have a blast and dance well into the night.

Potato Head Beach Club - Bali

Potato Head Beach Club makes its mark as one of Bali's prestige locations amongst some of the best restaurants, bars, and retail outlets. 'We wanted to create something original from Indonesia that could be seen and enjoyed by the Indonesian and international audience,' says co-owner Ronald Akili.

'The menus in Potato Head bistro are based on nostalgic home recipes and personal memories from our travels. We put our own collection in the restaurant, from the artwork to the furniture. We want people to see that we put our soul into each project and that we've invited them into our lives,' adds Ronald.

Since PHBC's opening in 2010, both owners have gained numerous international recognitions from various publications and media. Known for its multi-cultural blend of gastronomy, libations and entertainment which imbues music, art and fashion at the same time, PHBC has given Bali and its visitors the best of island living with a memorable and fun experience.

PHBC offers 3 restaurants, each presenting its own distinctive personality. Potato Head Bistro serves comfort food inspired by international home cooked recipes. Lilin offers a tapas selection of South East Asian cuisine and choices of exotic live seafood as its main highlight. The journey is not complete without savouring Chef Take's dishes made with passion and love.

Designed by acclaimed architect Andra Matin as a modern take on the Coliseum, the towering elliptical facade is crafted in Potato Head's seminal trademark of mismatched 18th century teak shutters collected from across Indonesia. The beachfront bar and 500 m2 emerald lawn leading to an infinity pool all fits within a state-of-the-art amphitheatre.

Covering three distinctly different dining options, lounge bar, infinity pool and a large lush grassed area, the entire place hums. At any one time there can be possibly 500 like-minded people enjoying the sounds from the resident DJ, who polishes the whole experience.

The tapas menu looks tantalizing, and the food arriving around you confirms it. The cocktail list is another story - new names, new mixes, new colours.

Prices - Berry Mule 100000 IDR (11 USD), Mojito costs 95000 IDR (10 USD). Booking essential.

Cuisines: Asian, French, International

Good for: Romantic, Bar Scene, Groups, Special Occasion Dining, Entertaining clients

Dining options: Breakfast-Brunch, Lunch Spot, Dinner, Reservations, Delivery, After-hours

Jenja - Bali

Jenja Restaurant, Bar & Club Lounge in the newish TS Suites Bali offers a one-stop evening out.

Located on Jalan Nakula, Jenja opens at 6 pm and offers a menu of exotic Asian and Middle Eastern dishes created by the winner of Top Chef Middle East 2012, the young Chef Selma AbuAlia.

The main dining area is also lined with comfortable sofas, serving those who prefer optional lounging with tapas and cocktails before heading down to the club. Chef Selma is boldly innovative, but with the menu at Jenja she retains some of her authentic Middle-Eastern flavours.

Regular DJs Mamsa, Wisdy and Heidy usually get started around 22:00 as the stream of w

Karma Beach - Karma Kandara
Karma Beach: Paradise with a new vibe

With blissful, barefoot days and carefree, glamorous nights, Karma Beach clubs aren't places simply to dip your toe in the water. Dive in for the ultimate in immersive, sand-and-surf hedonism.

Family-friendly, fun-filled days of watersports, beachcombing, oceanside spa treatments and cool, private cabanas, followed by sensual, star-filled nights with DJs, live music, cocktails and seafood feasts.

Karma Beach sets a new standard in chilled-out luxury in incredible locations, each with a unique vibe. It's time to join the club.

Motel Mexicola - Bali

Near La Lucciola and Petitenget temple, Motel Mexicola is a colourful Mexican bar and restaurant down Jalan Kayujati.

First you notice the colours and the atmosphere, then come the tequilas, margaritas and Cuba libres, and Corona. Savour Mexican tacos, tostadas, aguachile, quesadillas, antojitos (tapas). You may be fortunate to visit when Mexicola hosts one of its regular house parties with live Latin music.

The bunting of small red, yellow, green and blue flags strung across the street continues into its entrance, to a counter that serves Mexican drinks, tacos and fajitas. The cantina is a meeting point for those hooking up before going inside to party.

The courtyard is lined with bars serving shots and beer. The more sedate will want a more laid-back upstairs situation to relax and watch the ravers below. Enjoy the menu of affordable Mexican food before heading down to join the party. Opening Hours: 11:00 - 01:00.

Deus Cafe - Bali

Sticking up out of the rice paddies of Canggu and a stone's throw from Echo Beach, Deus Temple Of Enthuisasm houses a motorcycle workshop, surfboard shaping bay, artist studio, gallery, bar-restaurant and retail space. Deus makes motorcycles, Deus makes surfboards, Deus makes coffees, Deus is an afternoon outing in and of itself.

An awesome alfresco café serving up a range of delish food from the chef's specialty Thai to sandwiches and wraps and a unique kids menu. Never go hungry!

Cuisine: Asian, Barbecue, International, Bar.
Dining options: Breakfast/Brunch, Dinner, Late Night

Little rock 'n rollers, surfers, hungry ones, and Dads will dig it too!

Metis Lounge - Bali

The award winning 'MÉTIS Restaurant & Gallery' in Bali's jet-set Seminyak district are famous for their exquisite French cuisine, fine selection of wines and a gallery with the most impressive collection of contemporary and antique art. To further expand its already famous business, the Métis team are complimenting its roster with the opening of a new Lounge.

The new Lounge, designed by the famous Artalenta Indonesia, Architects and Interior Designers, is situated directly behind the restaurant overlooking a beautiful water lily pond and garden and features a truly unique and trendy ambiance.

The Lounge menu, distinct from the Métis Restaurant menu, is accompanied by an exquisite cocktail list using only high end spirit brands like Beluga

Vodka, Patrón Tequila, Dom Pérignon and Cristal Champagne. In addition to great cocktails and delicious tapas, a top-notch entertainment line-up gives the Lounge an international feel.

The high-tech retractable roof ensures that great times continue even during the short but unpredictable rainy season.

Managing Director Said Alem, says *'MÉTIS is always striving to innovate, while giving its customers the service and experience they're paying for.'*

With the new Lounge, MÉTIS offers a 360-degree concept that is one-of-a-kind in Bali and caters to all the latest trends. The venue offers the perfect start to a great night at MÉTIS Restaurant, or simply a stop-over while planning a tour of Bali's nightclub scene. MÉTIS Lounge is destined to be Bali's next 'not-to-be-missed' hotspot.

Single Fin

Uluwatu's legendary Single Fin started from humble beginnings and has quickly moved to the top of any Indonesian bucket list. Whether you're after an icy cold Bintang to celebrate an afternoon of long lefts, feel like kicking back to Wednesday's acoustic jams, need to jump-start your day with a Revolver coffee, or if you just really have to let your hair down with a few cocktails at Bali's most renowned Sunday session, Single Fin is the venue for you.

Boasting the biggest ocean side balcony in the archipelago, and possibly the most stunning views of one of surfing's spiritual homes, Single Fin comes alive as the sun sinks into the Indian Ocean. Great music (including regular international DJs and live acts), fantastic food and a laidback atmosphere make a visit to Single Fin a must-do for anyone who visits Bali, no matter if you're a frothing first-timer from far afield or a lifelong regular who grew up around the corner.

Double-Six Rooftop - Bali

Double-Six Rooftop, on the roof of Double-Six Luxury Hotel on the Seminyak beachfront, is designed, in the words of Robert Marchetti *'to blow our guests away.'*

Double-Six Rooftop is one of Bali's newest and most exciting drinks destinations, destined to be upfront on the growing list of Bali rooftop bars and restaurants, designed to take in the famous Bali views as well as ocean vistas.

15 meters above sea level, with stunning views over Seminyak's Double Six Beach. It covers 1700 square metres and it is one of the world's largest rooftop bars, boasting a five metre circular grill serving satay, 'floating' pods for drinkers and diners, and a mini-cinema.

Extending on the hotel's vision for the 'Living It All' destination, dining and entertainment, Double-Six Rooftop offer guests unique experiences of these forms of enjoyment in one venue.

Guests can savor locally inspired cocktails designed by Jonathan Jack, while listening to international entertainment acts and relaxing in 'floating' pods or private areas overlooking the Ocean.

The circular fire pit grill, where the 'United Flavours of Satay' are grilled over coconut shells and wood coals, creates a drawcard focal point in the centre of the rooftop.

The mini cinema, Pineapple Studios, will screen a variety of short films from the BALINALE: *Bali International Film Festival.* Guests will be able to wander up, pull up a deck chair, and watch some of the official selection.

Indonesian haute-couturier Chossy Latu's incredible theatrical costuming, with hostesses dressed in extraordinary head-dresses and gowns, as well as interior design features like the huge, shark and sting ray tank at the entrance will have guests staring in awe.

Double-Six Luxury Hotel and Seminyak Italian Food were created by a 'dream team' of the best Balinese and international creative minds, who have given the hotel its theatrical elements and high quality design so obvious in the innovative restaurant and bar offerings.

Spearheading the Double-Six Luxury Hotel, Seminyak team was Kadek Wiranatha, one of Bali's most respected entrepreneurs and hospitality leaders, responsible for creating well-known dining and drinking institutions including Ku De Ta, Chez GadoGado and Cocoon Restaurant and Beach Club. He was encouraged and assisted by renowned Australian restaurateur Robert Marchetti.

Marchetti says *'We really envisioned Double-Six as an entertainment precinct, a destination where people will come for some of the best drinking, dining and relaxing in Bali. I think the new Double-Six Rooftop Bar is going to be unlike anything else on the island of Bali.'*

Restaurants in Bali

Dining in Bali can be an exciting international adventure - beginning, of course, with Balinese Babi Guleng, or Indonesian Nasi Goreng or Mie Goreng. Then pick any letter of the alphabet and there is bound to be a nation with that letter listed.

Representing Europe you'll find France, Italy, Macedonia, Spain, Germany and many more. From the Middle East, Lebanon and other Arab nations offer their tasty dishes. Asia, of course, is best represented here, with Chinese, Japanese, Korean, Indian and Thai restaurants, either independent or within hotels. In fact, some hotels have restaurants representing as many as five different nations. If you want to really 'eat local', try one of the many 'warungs'. You won't be disappointed, and you may be shocked at how small the bill turns out when your meal is done. Often the food costs less than the drinks - that's just one of the delights of being in Bali.

Bridges

Set on seven levels overlooking the gently flowing Wos River, Bridges Bali is one of Ubud's premier culinary destinations. An ideal spot for memorable dining, a glass of wine with good friends or celebrating romance and to indulge yourself. A casual fine dining restaurant, wine bar and shop as well as exhibition and event space, Bridges Bali is where worlds meet.

Located in the charming village of Ubud at one of its most exotic locations, overlooking the tropical jungle and the Wos River, this riverside dining room offers delicacies from East and West. A finely crafted tasting menu is also available as well as a variety of vegetarian options.

Bridges is also home to Divine, Ubud's finest wine and cocktail bar down by the river. Enjoy great wines, amazing bar food and a spectacular view. The retail wine shop stock approximately 350 labels, one of Bali's most extensive wine lists.

Designed and built by Tjokorda Gede Oka Artha Ardana Sukawati (Tjok Ace) in a joint project with his brother Tjokorda Gede Putra Sukawati, the 27 years old restaurant was originally named Bridge Café. The multi leveled restaurant has witnessed the growth of Ubud over the years.

In 2008, the restaurant was handed over to the two oldest sons Tjokorda Gede Agung Ichiro Sukawati (Tjok Agung) and Tjokorda Gede Dharma Putra Sukawati, both of whom have graduated from universities abroad.

Honzen Japanese Restaurant - Bali

Honzen, one of several restaurants at Ayana Resort on the Bukit Peninsula (Uluwatu to most visitors) serves spectacular Japanese cuisine in a contemporary setting with Sushi & Sashimi Bar, Teppanyaki, Japanese Barbecue and Grill, and private Tatami rooms. Honzen offers a broad range of a la carte items in an ultra-stylish two-storey venue with indoor and outdoor seating, overlooking lush gardens and beautiful vistas.

Several different dining rooms with an outlook on one side to an open courtyard. The sushi/sashimi bar is an interactive experience. A very extensive menu, with illustrations that make it easy to follow. Certainly the sashimi is the highlight with the maki rolls, large but tasty. Contemporary Japanesewith Japanese music to help that ambience along. An experience not to be missed . Attentive staff open the doors and give a warm welcome.

Opening Hours: Lunch: 11:30-15:00 - Dinner: 17:30-23:00.

Bumbu Bali Restaurant and Cooking School - Bali

Do yourself a favour: escape the endless string of hotels and tourist restaurants serving up Western-inspired menus, and indulge in some of the best local cuisine around, at Bumbu Bali.

Slow-roasted chickens and ducks in banana leaves, freshly grilled seafood, sates, soups from banana stems, a satisfying selection of vegetarian dishes, Balinese cakes and seasonal tropical fruits are just a few of the island delicacies waiting to be discovered.

The menu at Bumbu Bali is the result of extensive research into the local food culture - including trips into many of the island's villages, homes and temples. All to bring you Balinese food prepared the way it is in homes, or for traditional ceremonies.

Corner House - Bali

Corner House, formerly The Corner Store has recently extended its hours to open for dinner. The cosy little gem has an unexpected package on offer. When you enter, check their daily specials on the blackboard.

You'll also find quiche, veggie burgers and a range of substantial salads on the menu. There is something for everyone, with children well catered for with a nice albeit limited kids menu.

Recommended: Corner House Burger (Rp 95,000), Fish & Chips (Rp 85,000) and Puff Pastry Quiche (Rp 52,000). Also lamb burger with minted yoghurt, balsamic glazed onion, cheese, cucumber and mixed greens.

They sell their own provincial style home wares range and stock Australian papers

Mama's German Restaurant - Bali

Operating as a #German-style bar and restaurant since 1985, Mama's is a hangout for travellers from all over the world, mainly Austrians, Swiss, Germans, Australians, but also Indonesians are enjoying the atmosphere and friendship made here. In the days when Bali's tourists were served Western food mainly in the form of Spaghetti and Pizza, #Mama's started a new trend, serving juicy real hamburgers (the owner hails from Hamburg, Germany) and hot dogs, with a decent portion of French fries. Soon original German style dishes were on the menu, such as: Roast Pork

(Schweinebraten), Vienna Schnitzel, Rolled Beef (Roulade) with Red Cabbage (Rotkol) and Bread Dumplings, all made at Mama's under the supervision of German Chefs.

Nowadays the choice includes many other wurst (sausages), Frikadellen (German meat balls), spit-roast chicken, pork roast, Rouladen (German beef rolls), and huge pork knuckles (Eisbein). To add to local draft beer, imported beers and German schnapps are also on tap, as well as a limited wine list. Diners may sit at the large tables and a bar downstairs or on the upper floor where there is a billiards table, and live music in the evening. Many tables are in true German size, 10 seaters for 'gemütlichheid'. Open 24-hours a day and 7 days a week.

The German Executive Chef and his crew prepare authentic #German, #European and #Indonesian #dishes in a nice atmosphere in the 'Dining Club' upstairs with a special Cocktail Bar. The area is ideal for private dinners, either just for two or for celebrations.

Taco Casa - Seminyak - Bali

Taco Casa's Commitment - Offer customers fresh, tasty food and beverages muy rapido y muy picante.

The Ingredients Matter - No matter if you are having tacos, burritos, enchiladas, fajitas, quesadillas, salad, fresh pure fruit juice or even a margarita, it is the ingredients that make the difference. It is what defines Taco Casa. That is why we take pride and great care in choosing the freshest and the bestest.

All made from Scratch - flour tortillas, guacamole, pico de gallo salsa, enchilada and hot sauce, beans, taco shells, corn chips, taco salad bowls and dressings are all made from scratch and contain no MSG or preservatives.

Open Daily 11 am - 10 pm

Ultimo - Bali

One of two sister restaurants of the Balinesia Company in the busy area of Seminyak-Kuta, South Bali, Ultimo Italian Restaurant packs authentic Italian food with affordable prices and a busy yet enjoyable atmosphere. Served in the traditional Italian style, the menu comes as a first course pasta dish followed by a main course of meats and fishes – not to mention the wide spread of pizzas, appetisers and desserts on offer as well.

The chefs use all the very freshest and finest ingredients to create an authentic Italian dining experience. Priding themselves on their high welcoming-factor, Ultimo is the ideal Italian restaurant for families and individuals alike. Guests can dine in the intimate dining lounge, or in the outdoor open air gardens (not to panic, there is air conditioning inside too).

Live music is put on regularly from Tuesdays to Fridays to keep the romantic/jazz vibe of the restaurant alive and there is also the opportunity for indoor and outdoor catering services provided for events and weddings.

Meja Kitchen and Bar - Bali

Meja Kitchen serves breakfast, brunch and dinner (7 am - 11 pm daily) inside or outside the space-age structure at IZE Hotel in Laksmana area of Seminyak. Meja, where friends or strangers come to meet, eat and talk around the table.

Australian styled food by Exec Chef Harrison - Duck confit, Truffle Mac and Cheese, plus much more Indonesian flavoured food.

The upstairs bar is akin to a laid-back Californian beach bar. Stools around the bar or low chairs around the scattered tables. Enjoy a wide range of snazzy cocktails, rum and whisky-based while you overlook the sights of Seminyak. The DJ deck is frequented by an international set of Disc Jockies. Bar open 5 pm - late Monday - Saturday

Sea Circus - Bali

Sea Circus is an odd name for a place that is not an actual circus and also not on the sea. It's kinda near the beach but as entertaining as a circus. In fact it's a really good Restaurant, Bar & Coffee Den thingy.

Acai berry: you can have your acai dose at Sea Circus Bali, packed full of antioxidants and tastes delicious. Best in the 'acai bowl' ensemble -- frozen banana, blueberries, acai and bee pollen served over Gypsy Lu's finest granola, topped with fresh banana, strawbs and bee pollen.

More super-grub:

Char grilled chicken, quinoa, yoghurt & beetroot relish.
4 crispy Balinese spiced tiger prawns, pickled palm hearts, chili & coriander.
Pan roasted barramundi, tomato & chili jam, couscous, fennel & coriander.
Baked parmesan dip with wild mushrooms, shallots, rocket & toasted sourdough.
Roast sirloin steak with oxtail potato croquettes, mustard crème fraiche & spinach.

Queens of India Ubud - Bali

In 2004 Queen's of India Jakarta extended its operation to #Bali, offering an extensive menu of authentic Indian cuisine, live music once a week, catering and free pick-up and return service for guests in the Ubud area. Each branch of Queen's Bali has a bar, an indoor air-conditioned dining area, an alfresco terrace, and an air-conditioned function room, but each presents different characteristics in keeping with its location.

Home delivery service at Queen's Ubud is provided by a dedicated motorbike fleet of delivery dispatchers. All orders delivered directly to your door within 30 to 45 minutes, depending on the area and access to the destination. Take-away food is carefully packaged in insulated, environmentally friendly, non-toxic, air-tight carry bags to ensure the optimum temperature of the food is maintained at all times so you can enjoy the freshest Indian cuisine at your villa, exactly as served at the table in the restaurant.

Dahana - Japanese Restaurant

Dahana is a family operated Japanese restaurant discretely situated in the heart of the culinary hub that is Petitenget. Separated from the hustle and bustle of the outside world by a softly lit ornamental pool, and surrounded by perfectly manicured gardens, Dahana offers a tranquil setting and comfortable space to cater for a relaxed culinary experience. The restaurant is set in an old villa which has been lovingly decorated with a modern yet cozy blend of old school Bali with a touch of Japan. The menu is a beautiful representation of various schools of Japanese gastronomy and the pricing is very reasonable. Dahana is a hit with the local ex-pat scene and is a beautiful destination for a dinner for two though more are welcome.

Taco Beach Grill - Bali

Come for a dip at Taco Beach ... 'Home of the original Babi Guling Taco!' where your vacation is on your plate. Unlimited salsa. Always fresh. Always free.

Choose from spicy, marinated carne asada tacos like those sold at Tijuana's roadside stands to 'Chipotle-Glazed Salmon Nachos with Cream Cheese and Leafy Green Herbs' on Bali's only hand-pressed, genuine Nixtamil Mexican corn chips.

Try original BaliMex fusion dishes, such as the savoury 'Babi Guling Taco' - chunks of roast suckling pig marinated in aromatic Balinese herbs and spices, and topped with homemade sour crema and your choice of fresh salsa.

Choice of original zesty salsas, like Mango-Lime, Tomatillo-Cilantro, Papaya-Pineapple, Chipotle Chile, Roasted Corn and Bean, Pico De Gallo, Roasted Red Pepper Guacamole.

Mexican favourites and Taco Beach originals in vibrant, colourful mixes of flavour and aroma.

Mades Warung Seminyak - Bali

The second Made's Warung, in Seminyak, has become a social eating and meeting venue for locals, expats and tourists alike. Nobody hurries off too quickly, the menu is that good. Besides local dishes like the iconic Nasi Goreng, sometimes with tasty extra ingredients, to curries, noodles (mie) and even choices for vegetarians.

Some items on the menu: Nasi campur, Nasi goring, Gado-gado, chicken, beef or pork sate, Tuna fish in Bali sauce, Lumpia (spring rolls), stuffed tofu shrimps, Mie kuah, Cap cay
Curry experts have a choice of curried vegetables, chicken, beef, crab, fish (ikan).

Vegetarians also have a large choice: Rujak, lumpia, fried green vegetables, gado-gado, full noodle list.

Kayuputi Bali Fine Dining Restaurant - Bali

of white, its décor a perfectly modern, elegant backdrop. Al fresco seating close to the sea means there is always a soft ocean breeze and an unobstructed view. Guests may reserve private cabanas for dining, or settle into a soft white cushion inside the high-ceilinged restaurant where the two-storey wine cellar and open kitchen add to the modern ambiance. The resort's sommelier is pleased to consult with guests on wine selections from our well stocked collection.

Inside the restaurant, an intimate bar area entices guests to a sofa deck and day beds, offering the perfect spot for the transition from day to evening cocktails before dinner. After dinner, enjoy the option of fine cigars from an elegant humidor.

Wacko Burger - Bali

Wacko Burger only works with the best ingredients, a juicy burger guarantee, straight from the grill. Wacko's chef works with a highly personalized herbal mixture, different each time, depending on the burger you choose.

From the classic to the most innovative creations there is a place for everyone's taste At Wacko we bring your imagination on a plate!

The bun, like a breast of an angel, relaxing softly on the delicious sauce beneath, aromas socializing in a seductive pas de deux. And then...a pickle! The supreme lively petite pickle! Then a slice of tomato and a crunch of onion, a foliage of lettuce and a patty of minced beef so superb, whirling in your mouth, breaking apart, and merging again in a fugue of sweets and savor so pleasing.

Drop. The Coffee Spot. - Bali

This attractive little café is the perfect place for people watching while sipping on a macchiato. Grab a stool outside and watch the world pass by There are great breakfasts, soups, quiches, and sandwiches but it's the Coconut Fluff that we recommend, a latte made with coconut milk.

With a drinks list as long as your arm, no one has ever gone thirsty here. Espresso. Cappuccino. Latte. Macchiato. Flat White. Lemonades. Juices. Chai. Herbal Tea. And they have a killer food menu too.

Take a seat inside or out for a big meal or small - this super cafe offers super affordable and totally delicious meals at a mere $6AU - $12AU.

You can expect anything from fluffy muffins to bright bruschetta and even sweet sticky crepes on the menu. Their homemade thin crust pizzas will satisfy even the fussiest eaters and they have salads for the health conscious.

Cafe des Artistes - Bali

Have a comfortable seat inside the main restaurant area or outside on our street-side garden terrace to enjoy a tasty meal, dessert or a well-made drink. Our ever-smiling staff will take care of you, in order to help make your visit an unforgettable one. Make your choice of any of our Indonesian dishes to have a taste of the archipelago or go for our grill-specials and western cuisine which features some Belgian specials as well.

For a lighter option our salads and snacks will be the right thing for you. Desserts a go-go for all the sweet-tooths as well as ice-creams and crepes. Check also our 'Monthly Special' out, a 4-course set-menu, designed to please your palate.

Chez Gado Gado - Bali

The alluring beach venue of Chez Gado Gado is an exotic blend of various elements resulting in a magical location with unsurpassed views to the Indian Ocean. The ambient décor and layout have been captivating and charming people for years, causing them to seek out the fine dining and distinctive wines.

Chez Gado Gado maintains its classic vibe and attention to detail, whilst it also provides a modern and contemporary environment that can cater for any function or event. The venue has evolved, but the menu has also gradually changed to reflect our customer's tastes and desires. Many old favourites remain, with an added new generation of specialities.

The cooking at Chez Gado Gado is based on using the best available produce from around Bali. Starters include crab ravioli, foie gras parfait, beef carpaccio, slow cooked prawns with Iberico chorizo. Main meals include poached coral trout, seared salmon, grilled tenderloin and twice roasted duck.

Happy Chappy - Chinese Restaurant

Happy Chappy is a convivial family-style Chinese restaurant inspired by a blend of traditional Chinese culture with a hip, modern influence. Make no mistake: Happy Chappy's whimsical take on upscale Chinese dining is tempered by one of the finest, state-of-the-art kitchens serving the most delicious traditional Cantonese-style Chinese food in Bali. Guests are delighted by Happy Chappy's inviting and contemporary environment with moderately priced, yet thoughtfully plated dishes.

The chefs at Happy Chappy have worked tirelessly to recreate favorite Cantonese-style dishes that westerners know and love. The food is simple and uncomplicated, made with fresh, high-quality ingredients – each of which evokes a nostalgia for childhood Chinese food delights. Family style servings make sharing part of the Happy Chappy experience – from the classic Honey Prawns to a spectacular Peking Duck. Drive-up take-away is also available so that guests may enjoy a delicious meal at their hotel or villa.

With a total seating capacity for 160 diners, Happy Chappy features a large and inviting dining area perfect for groups, families or couples. The old-shanghai inspired décor is contrasted by pops of modernity and elegance. Areas of the dining room can be configured to create additional privacy for large parties celebrating life's special events. The Fortune Pond, overseen by a life-sized statue of Happy Chappy, invites guests to drop in a coin and make a joyful wish to accompany their incredible meal.

The Dragon's Den bar is a chic lounge dripping in deep reds, evoking a feeling of mysterious decadence. This Chinese underground-inspired bar features one of Bali's largest live fish tanks to add an element of mystique to this mischievous side of Happy Chappy. Guests can indulge in an intimate conversation while sipping on a hand-crafted cocktail. The large outdoor patio area is perfect for enjoying Bali's gorgeous evenings under the stars. It's warm and upscale ambiance is the perfect place to enjoy a signature dim sum platter with group of friends.

Unique weekly specials and promotions keep guests returning multiple times during their visit to Bali and the quality and consistency of the food ensure that Happy Chappy is a must on any future trip.

Queens Tandoor Seminyak - Bali

Queen's is known for its professionalism, and for the high quality of its cuisine and service at most competitive prices. #Queen's Tandoor, Seminyak, #Bali invites you to join the thousands of satisfied clients who dine at our Indian Restaurant on a regular basis.

Considering a big gathering of 3000 people for a wedding reception, or a small gathering such as a birthday party or a reunion? Queen's have the expertise and enthusiasm to cater to the individual requirements of guests.

Home delivery is provided free of cost within a 15 km radius of Seminyak. QUEEN'S BALI home delivery is provided by a motorbike fleet of dispatchers. Orders are delivered to your villa within 30 to 45 minutes depending on area and access to your destination. Carefully prepared cuisine is specially packaged in insulated, environmentally friendly, air-tight carry bags to ensure the temperature of the food is maintained, so home diners can enjoy only the freshest Indian cuisine as you would expect to have served at the table in the restaurant.

Sangkar Restaurant at the Bulgari - Bali

In its breathtaking position at the edge of a cliff and with elegant yet informal atmosphere, enhanced by a magnificently illuminated ceiling and traditional woven lamps, the Sangkar Restaurant offers a menu of international specialities, creatively combining typical Indonesian dishes with contemporary culinary techniques. Open all day for guests to enjoy dishes such as tamarind chicken breast or bamboo shoot and vegetable curry with turmeric-scented rice.

Executive Chef Andrew Skinner suggests a selection of whole live lobster, an experience that will engage the senses and please the most discerning of palates.

USD130.00++ per person (subject to 21% government tax & service charge)

Sangkar Restaurant is also the setting for authentic Indonesian cuisine created by Executive Sous Chef I Wayan Wicaya - winner of World Association of Chefs Society (WACS) Global Chef's Challenge 2010 in Santiago, Chile.

Every day, starting from 6.30 p.m. guests will enjoy his 4-course menu, featuring Balinese cuisine at its best.

Taco Casa - Ubud - Bali

The Taco Casa Commitment - To offer customers fresh, tasty food and beverages muy rapido y muy picante.

Ingredients Matter - No matter if you are having tacos, burritos, enchiladas, fajitas, quesadillas, salad, fresh pure fruit juice or even a margarita, it is the ingredients that make the difference. It is what defines Taco Casa. That is why we take pride and great care in choosing the freshest and the bestest.

Made From Scratch - flour tortillas, guacamole, pico de gallo salsa, enchilada and hot sauce, beans, taco shells, corn chips, taco salad bowls and dressings are all made from scratch and contain no MSG or preservatives.

Cascades - Bali

CasCades restaurant has a little for everyone. There are elegant and traditional Balinese style pavilions, thatched wooden smaller pavilions or al fresco dining tables for a meal under the starry night sky. The grounds are nestled between jungle and farming land, with reflection ponds dotted about the place. Considered to be one of Bali's top dining spots. The tranquil oasis is a sought after location for an intimate meal, formal dinner or casual lunch. You can even get married there too.

With a relaxed and welcoming atmosphere, the staff at CasCades are committing to bringing you the very best service. With knowledgeable and friendly waiters, you are served your food with a smile. The dishes are produced using fresh and local ingredients of the highest quality. The cuisine is French inspired with an Asian edge, encompassing the 'lightness of Japanese, the aroma of Thai, and the careful consideration of Balinese spice'. There are three evening menus to choose from, as well as a breakfast menu and dessert menu. To see them all, .

Revolver Espresso - Bali

Revolver Espresso is one of the coolest coffee joints in Seminyak, Bali. If you love coffee, and enjoy cafe-hopping, you have to drop by Revolver for a cuppa when you are exploring Jalan Laksmana.

You will be hard-pressed to find Revolver Espresso unless you stumble on it entirely by accident, as they are tucked in a lane opposite the Bali Clinic and Zappa's. Alternatively, you can enter from the back of Home Store or This is a Love Song store.

They have by far the best coffee on the island and some amazing breakfasts like avocado on toast with a poached egg and a lovely cappuccino to start the day off well, and lunches too. The banana and peanut butter smoothie is brilliant. The decor is very quirky, cool and fun with some mellow funky tunes playing .

Like somebody commented: *The coffee here is fab. Don't bother polluting your body with coffee from elsewhere.* Cuisine: Café, Australian. Food options: Breakfast/Brunch. Price range: Rp. 35,000 - Rp. 58,000.

Weddings in Bali

Getting married soon? Wondered what a wedding on Bali would be like? Is it possible? Well, it IS possible and weddings have become part of Bali life. It matters not what faith, there are priests and imams, or civil officials who will do you the honours.

Many Bali hotels offer their services, and some have their own wedding chapels. They also have dedicated wedding teams who will arrange everything. All you have to do is see to a few documents in your home country. Dresses, suits, hairdo and make-up, ceremony, catering, flowers and transport will all be arranged, right down to (or up to) your elephant taxi to the altar in the case of Taro. Have a look through our wedding pages and see just what CAN be done to make your big day the most memorable event of your life, right on the sunny, beautiful, tropical island of Bali. Many hotels offer packages which include family members attending. You could even take over a complete collection of private villas and be very private - just a family affair.

Bali Good Food Catering - Bali

Greetings from BGF Catering.

Backed by the talent and experience of five of Bali's leading restaurants, and the bounty of our organic mountain farm, we offer both a variety of menus and a level of service that few can match. With hundreds of weddings, one Hollywood movie, and dozens of other events under our belt, we have earned our solid reputation for fresh and delicious food, beautiful setup, and warm caring service.

We also pride ourselves on our professionalism and high standards. Whatever your event, we know it is important to you, which means it is important to us. We want you to feel assured that it will be handled seamlessly by our experienced team.

Bali Elephant Safari Park Lodge - Bali

ELEPHANT SAFARI PARK WEDDINGS

The Elephant Safari Park has been voted as No.6 Most Unique Destination in the World of Weddings by Discovery Travel & Adventure Channel.

A Bali wedding and honeymoon is the ultimate romantic experience, especially if you arrive on a majestic elephant.

Bali Elephant Safari Park has a certain romantic mystique and aura that makes it a special place for weddings. Make your vows under a traditional antique four post decorative Javanese Joglo, a ceremonial pavilion featured in the palaces of the royal families of central Java.

The pillars are decorated with frangipani flowers and rose petals are strewn down the aisle to welcome the bride. The marble and stone Wedding Pavilion is positioned to feature a stunning backdrop of the elephant park. There is seating for up to 40 guests.

With the sun setting behind a beautifully carved white stone elephant altar and 30 ft high commemorative wedding flags, it is one of the most spectacular places to declare your wedding vows.

On your wedding night a candlelit romantic dinner for two is served in a privately appointed wedding gazebo.

We cater for small or large wedding receptions. Our restaurant overlooking the lake seats 200 guests.

ENTERTAINMENT

Music: Balinese Gamelan Instruments & Musician USD150 or Solo Violist USD600 or Solo Saxophonist USD600 or Accoustic Quartet Musician USD600

Traditional Balinese Dance: Traditional Balinese Dancer (3 Dances) USD200 or Kecak Dance USD800 or Jegog Dance USD900 or Legong Dance USD700

Photography and Videography

Wedding Photography for up to 3 consecutive hours photography session, including exclusive design photo album and 20 sheets USD800

Wedding Videography for up to 3 consecutive hours shooting and edited to 40 minutes footage.

Bali Catering Company - Bali

Bali Catering Company is the leading caterer on Bali, offering fine food, beverages and top quality service for weddings and events. Bali Catering Company is the frontrunner in gracious service, precision event planning and innovative cuisine.

Whether you are planning for a gala affair or an intimate family wedding, Bali Catering Company's well trained and experienced team are ready to help you with an event that will far exceed your expectations, captivate your guests and make for a truly unforgettable occasion.

Bali Catering Company's commitment to spectacular, unforgettable events never changes.

A good party is not about how much money you spend. It is style, taste and elegance that make the difference.

Over the years, we have had the privilege of working with a variety of people on a range of budgets to plan memorable events for thousands of pleasantly surprised guests. The freshest, most flavoursome ingredients are artistically prepared and presented with flair and finesse. Invitees are looked after with gracious, friendly, professional service at events which we have coordinated with unparalleled perfection.

Exceptional cuisine, blended with the magical atmosphere of Bali, will ensure that your dream becomes a reality. Our English speaking team have the experience and expertise, learned during years working in the luxury hotel industry, thus allowing our clients to rest assured that their celebration is in good hands, so they become a guest at their own party.

BEVERAGE MENUS

We offer various bar solutions, besides our ever popular 8 hours full open bar package. We also offer a Bar Upon Consumption with a wide range of spirits, wines and champagne. Beverage options are complete with bar accessories, equipment, structures, bartenders and service team.

We rent out chinaware, silverware, crystal glassware, tables and chairs for home celebrations.

We also offer wholesale prices for wines and spirits.

PREFERRED PARTNERS

Knowing that weddings have a host of details to consider, and that finding solutions in a foreign place with its own language and way of working may be complicated, risky and at times expensive, we have available partners with whom we work year after year.

Bali Weddings International was established fifteen years ago and is a member of the Association of Wedding Professionals International. Bali Weddings International and the Bali Catering Company combined offer you absolute perfection in the co-ordination and quality of your event.

Global Weddings Destination Wedding Specialists

Bali Exclusive Wedding Making every occasion exclusive

The Wedding and Events Specialist. A ONE STOP SOLUTION

Bali Wedding Butler - Bali

From the legal paperwork to commitment ceremony and finally the best celebratory party you could wish for, Desyana and her team could help you to arrange every aspect of your wedding and party

WEDDING VENUES

We cater for VILLA WEDDINGS at The Istana Villa - Atas Ombak Villa - Khayangan Villa

HOTEL WEDDINGS at Ayodya - Conrad - Ayana or Sunset Weddings at Melasti

WEDDING CEREMONIES

Moslem Wedding - Protestant Wedding - Catholic Wedding - Full Mass Wedding - Buddhist Wedding - Balinese Wedding - Civil Ceremony - Renewal of Vows - Commitment Ceremony

WEDDING DRESS

We are proud to provide wedding gowns both for local and foreign clients. Wedding dresses, traditional or glamorous, available to rent from our Wedding Gown

Gallery. We also offer 'Made-to-order' for special requests, which will be ready in 3 to 4 days.

WEDDING STYLING and MAKE-UP

Our Bali Wedding stylists and dressers offer many hair and make-up options, from Funky to modern or old-fashioned. You can use fresh flowers for your hair or just use a veil. Our stylist will come to your hotel or villa.

WEDDING FLOWERS

Wedding decorations with flowers from Bali are so beautiful. We can prepare wedding hand bouquet, flower posy, flower corsage, flower arch, standing flowers, dinner centre-piece and many other forms of floral decoration in Balinese or conventional style. As your personal wedding assistant, Bali Wedding Butler's florist will help you to achieve satisfaction with our colourful decorations.

Wedding Entertainment, Sound System and Lighting

Our professional team will orchestrate the finest entertainment for your wedding reception. Top Forty, Jazz or Blues, DJ, Batak string trio or quartet, modern dance (cha-cha, go-go girls show, firework dance and cabaret show), traditional Balinese entertainment (dances, gamelan, rindik, jogged, legong, kecak or ballet), even solo guitar or classical guitar. Dance till the morning, enjoying the night, welcoming the sunrise.... WEDDING FIREWORKS - Have a crazy party with simple or huge fireworks show, which will make your wedding unforgettable for everyone. We can offer many kinds of fireworks and include government fireworks permit.

Photos and Videos

Bali Wedding photographers take a different perspective of the wedding to capture the emotions and details that often go unnoticed. We can arrange both local and expatriate photographers for outdoor or indoor location shoots.

Wedding Cakes

We can provide any kind of cake. Choose from a wide variety of available styles, colours and flavours of cake, from one tier wedding cakes to 3 tier cakes. We are also able to make cakes based on your design even from a picture.

Wedding Gifts and Favors

Follow the traditional local culture by giving a unique gift by which each guest will remember your big day. A large selection of handicraft, wood carving, traditional dolls, mask, instruments, candles, aromatic oils.

You may need special HONEYMOON arrangements as well as holiday activities for your family and friends who have come over for the occasion, such as SPA and massage treatment, sport, golf, cooking classes, trekking, water sport, tours or other adventure experiences. We can arrange full programmes.

LEGAL WEDDING ARRANGEMENTS in Bali. Please see our site for all legal arrangements, including which of these we can process for you.

Testimonials

It is important that you have confidence in our ability to make you big day a success, so we offer you these testimonials

P.T. Tirtha Bridal - Bali

Tirtha Bridal is owned by Japanese husband and wife team Koji and Yuka Koreyasu, with the aim of creating unique and unrivalled weddings in Bali. The company employs more than 80 specialised personnel handling various wedding, function and accommodation ventures owned and operated by the Tirtha group.

9 years ago Tirtha Bali built a magnificent 6,000sqm, 15 pavilion Wedding Resort named Tirtha Uluwatu on the cliff-tops of South Bali, overlooking the Indian Ocean. TIRTHA ULUWATU was intentionally designed to host weddings that provide a sense of magic. One cannot quite describe the feeling of Tirtha Uluwatu, but, enter our property and you, too, will instantly know-- Uluwatu is a place like no other on earth for tropical

island weddings. The views, the architecture, and just the place itself evoke a sense of awe.

In 2005 Tirtha opened TIRTHA LUHUR, an exclusive three bedroom luxury private villa on 3,000sqm with a wedding pavilion, interconnecting indoor and outdoor dining locations, guest lounge and cloak room, swimming pool and gazebo, commercial kitchen and bar to cater to an elite group of bridal couples and their guests.

Enjoy your wedding--and First Night of your Honeymoon--at this most wonderful destination, the most luxurious wedding venue in Bali -- on the southern-most tip of Bali, within the intimacy of our secluded wedding villa.

The experience of Tirtha Luhur begins as soon as you move into the wedding villa, where every detail in the furnishings and accessories ooze luxury. Your waiting guests will be exploring the gardens and the total beauty of Tirtha Luhur. At the right moment, Balinese flower girls will escort you in procession to the Wedding Pavilion. In the evening of your new day as a couple, you retire to the wedding villa, enjoy a truly decadent bath, snuggle into the master bed, with richly appointed linens. Through the night and into the next morning prolong your blissful moments together.

Tirtha Bridal also has its own on-site BRIDAL BOUTIQUE, offering exquisite gift items, a wedding studio with 'off-the-catwalk' bridal dress designs, floristry, video, photography and banquet services.

Tirtha Bridal also arranges weddings in luxury five-star hotels and private properties in Bali. Tirtha has access to the island's best selection of entertainers, performers and event staff to create truly memorable occasions for any type of public or private celebration.

OPTIONAL OFFSITE VENUES

We have a partnership arrangement with the following hotels for hosting Tirtha-coordinated weddings:

The Four Seasons - The Legian - Bulgari Hotel - Alila Villas Uluwatu.

We can also provide wedding planning and coordination services for other hotels and villas in Bali.

Wedding Planning

Every Tirtha wedding is planned according to the unique personalities of each couple. At either Tirtha Uluwatu or Tirtha Luhur, you have almost unlimited options for expressing your preferences in colour scheme, table settings, candles, flowers, and other decorative items.

Styling and Make-Up

Not only do the staff at Tirtha Bali provide the most spectacular venue on the island, but we also have everything needed to perfectly adorn the bride and groom for their special day. We have a selection of over 500 gowns in many styles, and a wide assortment of matching shoes and accessories, to cater to your discerning tastes. Our professional staff and make-up artists will transform your casual arrival state into stunning elegance for your walk down the aisle.

The men's wardrobe includes the latest in tuxedos from Hugo Boss and other well-known fashion houses in Italy, with shoes and accessories to match

Stationery and Gifts

Express your appreciation for the commitments your guests have shown by providing customised items like special stationery for the wedding agenda, and seating and menu cards. And, since everyone loves receiving gifts, send them home with unique items that Tirtha can provide, such as Asian 'taste samplers' in wedding theme-inspired packaging.

HOTELS AND VILLAS

We have long-standing business partnerships with the following fine hotels and villas that entitle you to receive the best rates and conditions for your honeymoon in Bali.

Intercontinental Bali Resort - Conrad Bali - Ayana Resort - The Legian - Grand Hyatt -

Amanusa - Bulgari - Four Seasons Resort - St. Regis - Alila Uluwatu - The Bale - The Samaya - Kayumanis - Uma Sapna - The Elyssian.

Tokyo office - Tirtha Co., Ltd 6-8F

6-29-6 Shinjuku
Shinjuku-ku, Tokyo, Japan
Tel: +81 3 5447 2540
Fax: +81 3 5447 2558

Jimbaran Puri Bali Weddings - Bali
WEDDINGS IN BALI

Jimbaran Puri Bali presents a seamless planning service. Everything from commitment ceremony to a renewal of vows can be tailor-made. Choose between our two prime locations, with the sand between your toes in a barefoot ceremony on our tranquil beach, or stand under our intricate Puri Bamboo pavilion adorned with tropical flowers and romantic drapes within sound of the waves crashing on the beach just metres away.

WEDDING PACKAGES

- Let us take care of every detail of your wedding in Bali.
- Enchanting Wedding Package
- Make your day truly unforgettable with:
- A pre-wedding meeting with our wedding coordinator to discuss all your requirements
- An intimate ceremony by the beach or in the Puri Bamboo pavilion for up to 10 guests
- Exquisite decorations—choose between elegant Balinese or contemporary Western style
- An English-speaking Celebrant to lead the ceremony
- A delicate frangipani bouquet for the bride and boutonniere for the groom
- A symbolic marriage certificate

- A pillow for your wedding rings complete with decorative flowers
- Be serenaded by the beautiful sounds of traditional Balinese Rindik music throughout the ceremony
- Wine to toast
- Prices from US $1,490*
- Simple and Sweet Wedding Package
- For a more intimate experience we offer:
- An English-speaking Celebrant to lead the ceremony
- A beautiful ceremony by the beach or in the Puri Bamboo pavilion
- Simple yet elegant décor—a Balinese umbrella, walkway of frangipani, and fresh altar flowers
- Prices from US $700*
- Legal Wedding
- A legal ceremony with full documentation can also be arranged.

- We offer many more wonderful services, from photography to hair, make-up and cakes. For more information contact sales@jimbaranpuribali.com or complete our wedding enquiry form »
- Honeymoons in Bali

At Jimbaran Puri Bali honeymooners can revel in complete privacy in our haven of romance. Each of our luxury cottages and villas features its own walled garden and terrace. Laze on the twin hammocks under towering trees. Wander through the lush gardens. Take a sunset stroll along Jimbaran Bay's sands. Share a spa treatment in our specially designed spa terraces, separately or together. Enjoy an evening to remember with an intimate Duo Moonlight romantic dinner on the beach.

Mirage Chapel at Grand Mirage Resort - Bali

The Mirage Wedding in Paradise

Walk along the special white paved wedding way to the 'Mirage Chapel by the sea' with a gentle breeze through your hair and the sound of the Ocean ahead of you. The Mirage Chapel by the sea is the most open air dreamy and magical place for your wedding. Start with our basic wedding package and then add any optional services you wish.

We can prepare for a Catholic Religious Wedding Ceremony or a Protestant Religious Wedding Ceremony or experience the spirituality of a Balinese Blessing Ceremony at Grand Mirage Resort, with Balinese Costume and Culture on your unique and special day with traditional decoration, various offerings and prayers from Balinese celebrants for good things such as safety, health, bright future and happiness for the both of you.

Grand Mirage is an Indian wedding specialist and has successfully organized over 20 Indian style weddings over the past 3 years, each party having over 120 guests. They were very satisfied with our professional services. We have professional Indian Wedding specialists who will assist you with every step of your wedding, starting with the welcome parade to the final wedding dinner. We can tailor any custom plan to meet the exact needs of your Wedding.

We also cater for Balinese/Hindu, Moslem, or Buddhist style weddings

Your Wedding Date

The Wedding Ceremony can be arranged for any day of the week. The legal Wedding Ceremony might require extra efforts or extra charge if it is held on Saturday, Sunday or public Holidays.

Rendezvous Dinner

Private On The Beach in Your Cabana, for the two of you or with your friends and family. Let us arrange a memorable evening for the two of you. Don't miss the chance to spend one night under the stars with your feet in the sand and the sounds of the ocean.

for detailed prices on our large list of options, including special room rates for attending family, photographers, still and video, bridal dress and men's suit rental, hairdo and make-up, decorations, catering, drinks, dance band or Balinese musicians and much more. Couples wishing to get married legally in Bali whether local or foreign citizens, must firstly follow the religious wedding requirements. This is all explained on our site, as different religions have different requirements, besides the requirements of Indonesian law.

Conrad Bali Weddings - Bali

Whether you prefer a private garden gazebo surrounded by tropical palms and foliage or an oceanfront bale, a traditional Balinese pavilion, Conrad Bali's Wedding Specialists will help you create the Bali destination wedding of your dreams.

WEDDING VENUES AT CONRAD BALI

INFINITY CHAPEL

Our main wedding venue, situated in a private corner close to the beachfront. The chapel seems to be floating above sea level with an ensemble of overflowing reflecting pools and marble walkways. The interior is elegantly simple with marble floors, floor-to-ceiling ocean-facing glass frontage, and a seating plan for 60 guests. We offer 2 Wedding Packages at this venue:

Harmony Wedding Package

Hire of Infinity Chapel for one (1) hour; Use of bridal and groom preparation rooms two hours prior to wedding ceremony; Fresh flower decoration; Bridal bouquet and groom's boutonniere; Wedding celebrant; Music accompaniment by keyboard musician and singers; Conrad Bali's 'Bali Sunrise' signature wedding toast for up to 20 glasses (non-alcoholic); Commemorative wedding certificate and guestbook, presented in exclusive Infinity box; Conrad Bali wedding souvenir; Two (2) nights stay at Deluxe Ocean room including breakfast for bride and groom.

Splendour Wedding Package

Hire of Infinity Chapel for one (1) hour; Use of bridal and groom preparation rooms two hours prior to wedding ceremony; Fresh flower decoration; Bridal bouquet and groom's boutonniere; Wedding celebrant; Music accompaniment by keyboard player and singers; Conrad Bali's 'Bali Sunrise' signature wedding toast for up to 20 glasses (non-alcoholic); Commemorative wedding certificate and guestbook, presented in exclusive Infinity box; Conrad Bali wedding souvenir; Two (2) nights stay at Deluxe Ocean room including breakfast for bride and groom; Fireworks display consisting of 250 shots ; Contemporary dance as entertainment during wedding reception.

Infinity is available for wedding ceremonies at 10am, 11.30am, 1pm, 3pm and 5pm.

Water Garden

A unique Balinese pavilion floating in the middle of a lotus pond, provides a unique setting for your wedding.

The pavilion can be decorated in traditional Balinese or contemporary style. The two levels of grass terraces surrounding the pond can seat up to 150 guests. The Water Garden is available for wedding ceremonies at 10am or 4pm.

Floating Garden

A manicured lawn extending to a gazebo with a water fountain backdrop, the Floating Garden with a beautiful garden setting is a refreshing alternative to a beach wedding and can seat up to 140 guests. The Floating Garden is available for wedding ceremonies at 10am or 4pm.

Divine Wedding Package

Exclusive hire of Water Garden or Floating Garden for one hour; Use of bridal and groom preparation rooms two hours prior to wedding ceremony; Fresh flower decoration, in 'Contemporary' or 'Balinese' theme; Two Balinese flower girls; Bridal bouquet and groom boutonniere; Wedding celebrant; Musical accompaniment, choice of contemporary wedding singers or traditional Balinese 'rindik' music; Conrad Bali's 'Bali Sunrise' signature wedding toast for up to 20 glasses (non-alcoholic); Commemorative wedding certificate; Conrad Bali wedding souvenir; Two nights stay at Deluxe Ocean room for bride and groom.

Beach Bale

"Bale" is a traditional Balinese open sided gazebo with thatched roof of 'alang alang'. This is a perfect venue for those seeking a classic and intimate beachfront wedding. The Beach Bale is available for wedding ceremonies at 10am or 4pm.

Serenity Wedding Package

Similar to above, includes hire of Beach Bale for one hour; Traditional Balinese 'rindik' music accompaniment; A private five-course 'Romantic Dinner' at Beach Bale for bride and groom; Two (2) nights stay at Deluxe Ocean room for bride and groom

Wedding Reception Venues

Ocean Garden - A stunning 1,000m2 manicured lawn stretching to and overlooking the beach and Indian Ocean.

Infinity Garden - A private garden with Infinity as its backdrop.
Floating Garden - A manicured lawn with a water fountain backdrop.
Water Garden - A unique Balinese style pavilion afloat in the middle of a lotus pond, surrounded by manicured lawns.

Ballroom - Designed to host the most glamorous private events, The Ballroom opens to a garden courtyard and is supported by several smaller function rooms with complete audio- visual facilities.

Dijon Bali Catering - Bali

Catering at DIJON BALI covers a range of parties and weddings, brunches and lunches, cocktails and canapés or an exciting garden party barbeque! Most of all Dijon wants clients to have fun and feel satisfied after enjoying their amazing selection of food. Dijon Bali is a family run company and staff treat all guests like family. You will know that from their happy smiles.

At Dijon, the stock question is HOW CAN WE HELP YOU?

We were always about pleasing our customers and that is what we still focus on: happy customers. So our philosophy is Service First, personal service to guarantee customer satisfaction. We never stop trying to provide the best of a range of quality foods to meet the varied tastes of our diverse client base.

DIJON BALI opened in 1999 as the first gourmet delicatessen in Bali. No business supplied small quantities of anything in the gourmet line so we saw the need and opened in October. By Christmas 1999, the news had spread and DIJON BALI was the place to be. The rest is happy history.

Our Own Delicatessen Café
Visit the exclusive on-site lounge and café in Kuta to taste the gourmet menu of your choice. Dare to be

different! Taste our Balinese and Indonesian dishes. All food is sourced locally, if possible, except some foreign specialities like smoked salmon from the cold-water seas. Shop Hours: Mon - Sat 9 am to 9 pm - Sun - 10 am to 9 pm

Service Deliveries....?

We provide chilled delivery service to many central areas of Bali, with only a small minimum charge. Three times a week our refrigerated truck goes to customers in Ubud. Long distance customers can order, pay by transfer and have their special goods shipped to their home or party venue. We happily wrap things for gifts or shipping and can order dry ice for those who request it. Yacht owners can order and have their food delivered to their mooring by appointment.

PACKAGE DEALS

3, 4 or 5 Course Set Menu - Western Buffet Menu - Barbeque Menu - Canapes Menu -Children's Menu - Indonesia Buffet - Drinks Pack

DIJON Catering Bali organizes parties and weddings in many sizes and types. For additional information, contact Mr. Frank at frank@dijon-bali.com

Simply Yours Wedding Caterers - Bali

Lynley Marston offers a wide range of Bali wedding venues, lighting, entertainment and delicious menus to celebrate your memorable experience in your own unique style. She is there on your wedding day to make sure everything goes according to plan. Lynley ensures all the pre-planning efforts come to fruition in a flawless event that you and your guests will treasure forever.

With over 35 year's experience in culinary art and her skilled coordination of events, Lynley recently added Madison Setiawan to her team to form Simply Yours, an affordable wedding alternative with the same quality and personalised touch on a fixed budget.

Simply Yours budget wedding packages include catering, venue, accommodation, floral and decor and the ceremony. For a taste of what your dream event can look like, managed by Madison and Lynley, download Simply Yours budget wedding brochure and you're one step closer to the magical event of your dreams at an affordable cost.

Combine perfect exotic cuisine with an idyllic tropical atmosphere and location and serve it with exceptional service - these are all essential ingredients to Lynley's catering and events success. Nothing is neglected when it comes to exotica, creativity and imagination. Organizing an event from 80 to 500 never phases Bali's most sought after hostess. Lynley is a friendly professional, who combines creative talents with flawless organization to bring every event vision to life.

Boutique Catering

With a large selection of menus being constantly reviewed and updated, Lynley will guide you through the variety, style and pricing for your special event. Choose a menu from one of her existing packages or feel free to create a menu of your own.

Lynley's trained cooks will prepare stylish and contemporary food, fresh in quality and seasonal in trend. Lynley has flexibility to work within a budget, the desire to excel and the imagination to offer something a little bit different.

Lynley is there on your wedding day to make sure everything goes to plan so all you have to do is enjoy yourself. She ensures all the pre-planning efforts come to fruition in a flawless event that you and your guests will treasure forever.

Unique Venues

Lynley's selection of unique Bali venues will impress anybody. She has a direct line selecting and securing Bali favourites. Whether you are looking for a boutique resort, a luxury villa estate or a stunning private beach-front location, Lynley will find the perfect place to match the perfect celebration.

Heliconia Floral Art - Bali

Gede Arya approached Australian Michael Pritchard to put his more than 20 years experience in the flower industry in Sydney, into the formation of a team of talented designers to create interesting and unusual floral designs for the Bali and Indonesian market. Most of the flowers used by Heliconia are grown in Indonesia, but some exotic blooms are also imported for a particular function or client, often using fresh bamboo, natural or sprayed, with tropical fruits and unusual combinations of natural material.

Innovative floral designs by Heliconia have set the standard for the flower industry in Bali and beyond, with extensive experience in organizing and orchestrating world class events and creating personal themes for special functions.

Local clients include Ku de ta, Papparazzi, Double Six, Bacio, Living Room, Westin Hotel, Como Shambala Estate, Four Seasons and Nikko Hotel. The team arranged flowers for the former president Megawati Sukarno Putri. The Australian Government chose

Heliconia to design the site and create the floral decoration for the first anniversary of Bali Bombing in 2003 which included guests from all over the world. Heliconia supply most of the top end private villas and handle most of the large events and weddings in hotels on Bali.

The design team was chosen by Indigo Pearl – a boutique hotel in Phuket, Thailand in November 2006, completing the training of the floral department of this luxury boutique hotel (300 rooms) including setting up a retail gallery style flower shop in the lobby, back of house flower department and flower designs for all public areas, rooms and spa.

The team visited the Park Hyatt in Goa, India in January 2007 to organise their in-house flower department, covering all room flowers, as well as public areas and restaurants.

Heliconia's approach to floral art is contemporary and each design is a one-off creation that can stand as an art form on its own. The design team is continually searching for new inspiration and ideas with the stress on individual creativity within the team.

Courtyard Weddings at Nusa Dua - Bali

Marriott's Courtyard Bali Nusa Dua hotel is situated in a luxurious and safe enclave on the stunning coast of South Bali's Bukit Peninsula, minutes away from the tranquil and pristine white sand beaches. This paradise destination within a 350 hectare purpose-built holiday estate, is perfect for those wanting romance, relaxation or a peaceful honeymoon. Have fun in our lagoon swimming pool, pamper yourself at our health club or spa, or take romantic walks along miles of white beaches and enjoy the private Beach Club. If you are open to exploring Balinese culture, then local cuisine, shopping and entertainment can be found at the Bali Collection in Nusa Dua, where connecting with the Balinese people is a pleasant experience.

Nearby attractions, Waterboom Park, Benoa Marine and a championship 18-hole golf course are sure to please any outdoor enthusiast or adventure seeker. Beachside and water sports are just minutes away. With so much to explore, our Bali hotel is the perfect venue for weddings and honeymoons to capture the splendour of the Paradise Island of Bali.

Meeting-Reception Rooms

- Our Reception Rooms have the following capacity Reception Banquet setting
- Palma 374 persons 218 persons or divided into
- Palma 1 187 persons 109 persons
- Palma 2 187 persons 109 persons
- Krisan 329 persons 192 or divided into
- Krisan 1 110 64
- Krisan 2 110 64
- Krisan 3 110 64

TYPES OF GUEST ROOMS

- Deluxe, Guest room, 1 King or 2 Double

- Deluxe, Guest room, 1 King or 2 Double, Pool view
- Premium, Guest room, 1 King, Corner room
- Deluxe Terrace, Guest room, 1 King or 2 Double, Poolside view
- 1 Bedroom Suite, 1 King, Poolside view

Courtyard Spa

Body scrub, Body wrap, Couple's Massage, Facials, Fitness classes, Foot bath, Kids Services, Makeup Services, Manicures/pedicures, Massages, Men's services. Appointment is required. Phone: 62 361 300 ext. 8728

Health and Fitness Centre

Cardiovascular equipment, Free weights, Body treatments, massages and spa packages available. Fitness services: Spa features dual massage suites

Weddings at The Laguna Bali - Bali

Each one of the timeless western or Balinese style wedding packages on offer is impeccably designed down to the very last detail, including legal registration for couples and a wide variety of party, dinner and celebratory options. Combined with the assistance of on-site wedding specialists, an unforgettable and stress-free affair is guaranteed. Your romantic journey begins with a personal selection from one of the enchanting wedding venues, architecturally crafted to complement the resort's natural beauty.

The Laguna Gazebo
The Laguna Gazebo offers an unrivalled beachfront location overlooking the sparkling Indian Ocean. Alluring and intimate, the gazebo exudes tropical sophistication, enchanting you and your guests with authentic Balinese touches that include a romantic alang-alang thatched roof, an eclectic mix of timber and marble flooring, welcoming earthy accents and lush, exotic greenery.

Nusa Bagus Island
Nusa Bagus Island is an exclusive and intimate venue, surrounded by water features and offering captivating

views of our turquoise lagoon. A tranquil waterfall provides a relaxing and soothing backdrop, perfect for your dream wedding ceremony.

Temple Garden

The Temple Garden promises to add a sacred touch to your wedding ceremony, allowing you to truly immerse yourself in one of the island's most enchanting wedding venues. Romantically set amid the true elements of Bali, a stunning Balinese temple creates an unforgettable cultural ambience.

Beach

Internationally renowned as one of the most stunning white sand beaches in Asia, the dramatic beach cove at Laguna invites pure island romance and one of the most memorable wedding seascapes in Bali, realising your dream of a beachfront wedding in paradise.

Secret Garden

Secret Garden is a hidden gem, hidden in the lush foliage amid the exclusive Laguna Pool Villas. Offering an expansive green lawn surrounded by flowering trees, a picturesque waterfall is the ultimate romantic accessory.

Westin Resort Wedding Planners - Bali

In your romantic dreams, shared with your lover, you decided to look at Bali, famous for ages as an island of blissful romance and exotic intimacy; and you were right: Bali could and will provide an exquisitely perfect destination for any dream wedding. Now think Nusa Dua and The Westin Resort, part of an international group with dedicated wedding organisers and local experts who will plan your every need and desire with you.

Think of delightful sunrises and sunsets and tropical white sandy beaches with swaying palms, painting it all elegantly into your memory with soft touches of Balinese hospitality and genteel service. Then add excellent local and international food and you could have the perfect wedding. You and your family or guests could all stay within the enclave of Nusa Dua, with its top range of 5 star and 4 star resort hotels, secure and peaceful, with so much for a newly married couple to do, if they so wish, or to just laze on the beach or beside our fresh water and salt water pools.

The Westin Resort Nusa Dua offers several wedding venues, each with its own unique personality and cachet. The white sands of Nusa Dua always manage to win hearts as a venue to toss a wedding bouquet. The moonlit Balinese limestone pool area, By The Water, casts a spell with floating candles and bougainvillea cascades of colour. The gilded atmosphere of the Nusa Indah Hall wraps guests in hushed luxury as the bride and groom walk down the aisle. We can cater for a thousand guests or a few or just the two of you. The resort's skilled staff and associates will turn any couple's special day into a dream to remember forever.

Then look at the enormous number of activities going on all over Bali, from stunning theatre shows within Nusa Dua, to thumping nightclubs in Kuta, to placid waters or roaring surf; from luxury boat excursions to nearby Nusa Lembongan or Nusa Penida, to underwater sight-seeing in a real mini-submarine specially fitted for viewing the stunning array of undersea life around Bali's coast. Or visit the green hills around and north of Ubud.

From March 2013 you will even be able to overnight at our new Westin resort at Ubud and take in the local scenery, from terraced rice fields to looming volcanoes and placid lakes, from ornate temples to bustling fruit markets, where you will see fruit that you have never seen before. Your honeymoon on Bali will never have a dull moment.

CATERING

A vast choice of creative cuisine, ranging from Indonesian to Japanese, Indian and Western meals, arranged by the hotel's renowned culinary team, is available to suit everyone's taste, including a rich selection of hors d'oeuvres and super-sized cocktails, scrumptious buffets and elegant course-by-course meals.

The Westin Resort Nusa Dua, Bali guarantees to make wedding planning a hassle-free process. Everything from décor, flowers, photography, music and even the Balinese flower girls are arranged so that the couple can relax and simply enjoy their day.

Our experts will also advise you what to bring in the way of paperwork, so that the formal side of your wedding proceeds without problems. We are able to arrange Catholic, Protestant, Hindu and Muslim weddings with ordained celebrant, or simple civil or humanist weddings.

Contact our Wedding Specialist
at wedding.specialist@westin.com

Have a look at our Resort and its facilities on this site: The Westin resort Nusa Dua Bali. You may also see a list of Indonesian wedding requirements on this site.

The Beaded Boudoir - Bali

European-style wedding gowns at a fraction of the price paid in Europe, designed by Sandra at The Beaded Boudoir. You could find yourself a fabulous couture wedding dress, normally only available in countries like Italy and France for thousands of Euros. Have it adjusted by Sandra and staff to suit you perfectly, made to measure, and pay Bali prices.

The glittering salon, which partially occupies the property of owner Sandra McArthur, is filled with fabulous custom-beaded handiwork. She stocks dresses, suits, and evening gowns embellished with all manner of sparkling beadwork: everything from Swarovski crystals to glass beads, and sequins to pearls and seashells.

Your wedding is a once-in-a-lifetime experience. Let Sandra dress you and make you feel like a princess on your wedding day. When last did you have the opportunity for a private session with a top clothing stylist? THIS is the time you should have your first 'experience'.

Sandra will prepare your dresses, not only wedding ceremony dress or gown, but also dresses for 'pre- and post-wedding events' which are more opportunities for you to look spectacular and feel incredibly spoiled.

Sandra can create for you an entire bridal party ensemble, bridesmaids and flower girls included, to look and feel the part on your big day. Imagine sharing your photos with your future husband and family and your future children one day, and the gasps of admiration your spectacular photographs will engender.

Let Sandra also dress the Mother of the Bride and give her the opportunity to look and feel wonderful on her daughter's special day. With gowns, long and short dresses, pants and tops to select from there truly is something for every lady involved in your wedding ceremony.

Your visit to Beaded Boudoir will be yours alone, with attention given only to YOU when you make an appointment with us. Of course you may bring someone with you if you wish. However, no more than 3 may be included in a session with Sandra. That way you will have Sandra's complete focus and attention, to really experience having `my own private stylist'.

"The Beaded Boudoir is the most gorgeous sparkling boutique of its kind. Couture made in Bali, shipped to Italy with an occasional one-off garment ending up in the Beaded Boudoir. So if you want to feel beautiful, then Sandra is the person to give you that belief in yourself - especially when you are paired with a dress that fits your style, personality and body, all at the same time."

Dini's Bridal - Bali

Dini's Bridal, established in 1996, provides a bridal service, renting bridal gowns and tuxedos, preparing bridal makeup and hairdo's in a special makeup studio, using professional equipment, and original International products. Dini is an accomplished wedding gown designer, make-up artist and hair stylist.

Dini has been breaking new ground year after year in the field of fashion, makeup and hairdo, participating at the International level fashion show 'Bali Fashion Week' , a spectacular single show of wedding gowns and salons in 2002, 2003, 2005, 2009 and 2010 (Mall Bali Galleria).

PORTFOLIO

- ➢ The best 10th of Bridal make up 'Perkawinan Magazine' Jakarta, 2001.
- ➢ 1st winner evening makeup, Tiara Kusuma, Jakarta 2002
- ➢ Spectacular Bridal Show and Exhibition at Mall Bali Galeria in 2002, Bali.
- ➢ Bridal show 'Glorious of Egypt' at Bali Galeria in 2005

- Bridal Show La Tulip at Tiara Dewata Bali in 2006
- Spectacular Bridal show at Water Bom Bali, 2007
- Spectacular Bridal and Hair show 'Rhythm in Sahara' 2008
- Spectacular Bridal and Hair Show featuring Dian Sastro & Loreal Professional Indonesia, Bali in 2009.

Special Services

Using a selection of high quality product such as MAC, Dior, Channel, Bobbi Brown, Lancome, Estee Lauder, Giorgio Armani, Shiseido cosmetics, Versace. All products have been allergy & ophthalmically tested.

- Our Services :
- Western Expert hair and make-up by Dini
- Western hair and make up by professional make-up artist (assistance)
- Hair Styling only for Bride

- Western Expert hair and make up by Dini with Air Brush
- Make Up only for Bride
- Touch up for Bride after ceremony
- Hair and Make-Up for Photo Tour
- Additional extension per hour for photo tour
- Additional Hair Styling only for Groom
- Additional hairdo and make up for Groom
- Additional Trial hairdo and make up for Bride
- Retouch hairdo and make-up for Bride
- Additional Hairdo and make up for guests

Seventh Heaven Weddings - Bali

Khayangan Estate, at the southern-most tip of Bali Bukit Peninsula, represents the best in Bali villas and is an unsurpassed venue for your tropical wedding. Khayangan means 'Seventh Heaven', a highly appropriate name for this Bali tropical wedding venue. The stunning 15000-square-metre Khayangan Estate presents a beautiful cliff top garden, 170 metres above the rolling surf of the Indian Ocean, where frangipani trees drop their scented flowers on the manicured lawns, and two large balé pavilions provide a comfortable space for guests to lounge in opulence. Balinese ceremonial 'umbul umbul' flags flutter in the gentle breeze, red bougainvilleas add a splash of colour, and the rhythmic sound of the waves reminds you that you are in a very unique palace garden.

Can anything be more romantic than tying the knot with the one you love upon the breezy Khayangan cliff top against the spectacular backdrop of the Indian Ocean? Whether you are planning an intimate sunset ceremony or a lavish celebration with family and friends, we will make sure that your dream becomes a reality. As one of the best Bali luxury villas, Khayangan Estate have the expertise to create an unforgettable ceremony that you will treasure for the rest of your lives.

Our specialist tropical wedding caterers will delight you with their stylish, artistic expression. The freshest, most flavoursome foods are carefully prepared and presented with flair and finesse, while guests are looked after with gracious, friendly, professional service. The wedding banquet could be a sumptuous four-course dinner, a barbeque of fresh lobster and seafood, or an enticing feast of local Balinese delicacies. This will be further enriched by a colourful tailor-made tapestry of flowers, linens, candles, ice sculptures, musicians, fire-dancers and Balinese dance troupes, against a backdrop of natural tropical décor.

Our florist will arrange magnificent tropical flower displays which might include elaborate two-toned heliconias and sweet smelling 'sedap malam', with carpets of rose petals, Meduri flower curtains threaded with sweet scented wildflowers, bamboo archways of trailing palm fronds, flaming torches, fire-bowls and floating candles. The Balinese are experts at ritual and ceremony. One only has to witness some of their lavish Hindu festivals and celebrations, suffused with the clever use of natural materials such as bamboo, palm leaves, flowers and fruit, to get an idea of the potential that Khayangan has to offer.

As each bride wants to look her most beautiful on her wedding day, a range of professional hair and make-up services are available for the bride and attendants. Our associated specialist bridal boutiques present a wide selection of wedding dresses and men's attire in a range of sizes, for the bride, groom, family and guests, including designer labels. To make your tropical wedding even more romantic, you and your guests may be dressed in traditional Balinese costume. Bride and groom can be dressed in resplendent gold and red cloth, with the bride wearing an ornate golden headdress garnished with jasmine flowers to represent the rays of the sun.

The elegant private garden, dotted with terraces of pretty yellow irises under swaying coconut palms, offers an amphitheatre-style terrace that can accommodate several hundred guests – perfect for an open-air Champagne reception. The recommended time for a wedding ceremony is around four or five o'clock in the afternoon, when the heat of the day has subsided but there is still enough light left for taking stunning sunset photographs within an enchanted setting. A culmination of this wedding made in "Seventh Heaven" would be a bountiful marriage feast, followed by a candlelit alfresco fiesta.

Khayangan Estate offers tailor made wedding packages to suit every need and fulfil every dream. We will introduce you to specialist wedding planners who not only coordinate the legalities for the ceremony, but also provide the services of professional celebrants, photographers, videographers, musicians, dancers, florists and caterers; everything will be taken care of right down to the invitations, the stationary, the hair and make-up, the decorations, the bridal gown, the guests' costumes and the cake.

Khayangan is a fully SELF-CONTAINED PRIVATE ESTATE with its own security staff. We offer

Six ultra-lavish bedroom suites with the most romantic en-suite bathrooms that you will find anywhere in Bali luxury villas.

- Two grand living and dining pavilions.
- Two large infinity-edge swimming pools.
- A professionally-equipped spa.
- A cliff-top relaxation pavilion.
- A fully equipped modern kitchen.

See photos, below, of our SULTAN MASTER SUITE, MAJAHAPIT SUITE, our ornately decorated KERATON SUITE and our magnificent and palatial MAHARAJA SUITE.

All this within a self-contained and walled Private Estate, ideal for a very personal and yet memorable family wedding.

REASONS FOR CELEBRATING YOUR WEDDING AT KHAYANGAN

The Villa Estate is remote, quiet and private. You will not "disturb the neighbours" with your wedding music.

It also has its own security guards, which is a vital factor for celebrities and elite travellers.

The Villa Estate uniquely designed, made up of ten antique wooden houses from Java. These were once the homes of noble men. They have now been adapted to suit the modern world. These grand old houses will take you back through history to a time of finery.

These cliff top luxury villas are furnished with pure comfort in mind, set in a lovely garden, with sweet scented trees, flowers and swaying palms. All of this looks out over the vast Indian Ocean.

The most luxurious villas - Each bed is set within a nest of wooden pillars and nets. The beds are topped with richly carved wooden tiers. The bedrooms have king-size beds and best quality cotton bed linen.

The most exotic bathrooms in Bali

Two of the suites have the most romantic bathrooms that you can imagine. A covered bath tub floats in the middle of a clear pond, beside a waterfall and a lush garden.

Five star villa service - Twenty four hour Butler service. The service given by these highly trained young men and women is perfect, yet it comes from their hearts.

The Spa on the edge of the cliff is fully air conditioned with all facilities. This includes a steam room, hot tub, and cold plunge pool by the edge of the cliff.

Dominic Vanyi Artistic Photography - Bali

Its multitude of stunning locations, unique architecture and enchanting culture have made Bali Asia's prime location for couples seeking to celebrate their union in marriage. Dominik Vanyi of Denpasar in Bali is an award winning international wedding photographer who also produces stunning pre-wedding photography. Dominik is responsible for over 300 successful couples showing off their wedding albums to family and friends. He offers a range of attractive packages and photo tours around the island. He also does family portraits and child photography.

Austrian-born Dominik is rated as Bali's best wedding photographer and, in over 8 years, he has photographed weddings in Bali and international destinations beyond Bali. He will provide you with an outstanding collection of natural looking, non-posed photographs, which will highlight the uniqueness of your wedding.

Although Dominik has been chosen to do many industrial and shipping photos, wedding photo-journalism and candid photography are his hallmark. His work has appeared in many magazines, winning him international awards. A keen eye for the defining moments and the heartfelt emotions of your wedding make him stand out among Bali wedding photographers. Ask Dominick for the most discerning documentation of your wedding in Bali and he will "produce the goods" as the many photos on his website, www.d-weddings.com/contact/ will prove.

Have a look at Dominik's portfolio which covers in excess of 300 weddings. For an easy viewing experience of the weddings covered, they are sorted by type of wedding. Dominik emphasizes that it is people and their heartfelt emotions that are the main focus of his work, regardless of the location. For more information on Real Weddings in Bali make sure to check out also Dominik's Blog, www.bali-wedding-photo-blog.com/ where you can also read relevant and inspiring information about those weddings in the many lovely testimonials from satisfied clients.

Dominik Photography works with Baliku Weddings, Bali Wedding Paradise, Bali Mystical Weddings, Bali Wedding Experience, and others. Dominik's preferred partner for make-up and hair styling services is Bali Make-up & Hair. The sister company for services for local, professional wedding photography is Wedding Photography Bali as well as www.weddingphotographybali.cn for clients from

China. His team also does wedding videos as part of Dominik's service offerings.

Dominik's photographs have appeared in many national publications such as Wine&Dine, Hello Bali, Belladonna - The Wedding, Bali BITE and others.

Dominik was the only international photographer featured in American style guru Susie Coelhoe's wedding book: Style your dream wedding. Australian publications that have featured Dominik's photographs are: Australian Bridal Magazine, Bridal Options, Holiday for Couples and others. Photographic assignments have taken Dominik to Perth – Australia, Hong Kong, Malaysia, Singapore and China.

Lastly Dominik is also an accomplished fine-art photographer and has exhibited his work in Jakarta and Bali. For more information on his fine-art photographs and books please refer to: www.d-fine-art.com

Dominik is a proud member of the GUILD of Bali Wedding Professionals.

Epic Photography - Bali

Bali is one of the most amazing wedding destinations in the world! With an abundance of stunning locations, amazing beach backdrops, dramatic clifftop villas, lush green forests and perfect weather, you will be spoiled for choice when designing your dream wedding in Bali. To make sure you don't miss a moment, a laugh, a tear, the fun, the ridiculously beautiful scenery and the emotion of the most amazing day of your lives you need the best, award winning Bali wedding photographer, Chris Garbacz from Epic Photography!

He is a fun, easy going photographer with plenty of experience to get the best out of you on your very special day.

Bali Limousine - Bali

Bali Limousine is a car rental company offering exclusive automobiles with driver. Our services cover from airport-hotel transfers or city tours to business meetings, congresses, conventions or weddings.

Indonesia Information

Bali Limousine is a centrally located in the traditional village of Ubud, Gianyar. We pride ourselves on personal service, well-maintained, safe cars and an extensive knowledge of Bali. When you rent a car from BALI LIMOUSINE, you are not just renting a car, but joining a new family of friends on Bali. Owner and operater Wahyu Sudarmana of Bali Limousine has been serving locals and tourists on Bali for more than five years.

With so many opportunities for fun, adventure and beauty, it can be overwhelming to plan the perfect vacation to the Island. Bali Limousine is here to help. We are always happy to share our insight and experience, to ensure you have a truly wonderful stay here. Come and join us in discovering and exploring the real Bali, The Paradise Island of Indonesia.

The staff at Bali Limousine relies on feedback from our past customers, so we can offer suggestions for the perfect Bali experience. We are proud of our close relationships with our customers and are more than happy to take the time to answer your questions.

CARS FOR HIRE

- ✓ Hummer H2 Limo
- ✓ Year 2010. Capacity 15 passengers.
- ✓ Full day (10 hours): IDR42,000,000
- ✓ Rental per hour (Minimum 3 hours): IDR4,800,000
- ✓ Extra time per hour: IDR4,2000,000
- ✓ Mercedes Benz C Class C200
- ✓ Year 2010, Capacity 4 passengers
- ✓ Full Day (10 hours): IDR2,160,000
- ✓ Extra time per hour: IDR216,000
- ✓ Toyota Alphard Vellfire 2010
- ✓ Capacity: 6 passengers
- ✓ Full day (10 hours): IDR2,400,000
- ✓ Extra time per hour: IDR300,000
- ✓ Ferrari California

Indonesia Information

- ✓ Year 2010. Capacity: driver + 1 passenger
- ✓ Full day (10 hours): IDR78,000,000
- ✓ Rental per hour (Minimum 3 hours): IDR8,400,000
- ✓ Extra time per hour: IDR7,800,000
- ✓ BMW Z4
- ✓ Year 2005. Capacity: driver + 1 passenger
- ✓ Full day (10 hours): IDR4,800,000
- ✓ Rental per hour (Minimum 3 hours): IDR1,200,000
- ✓ Extra time per hour: IDR480,000

Our specialised Car Rental with Driver services include :

- ➢ Limousine service
- ➢ Transfer Airport to Hotel to Airport in Bali
- ➢ Official car service for companies
- ➢ Escort service for weddings and ceremonies
- ➢ VIPs escort service
- ➢ Guided tours of the most famous Bali sights

Bali Wedding Planners - Bali

Thinking of getting married on Bali - The Paradise Island?

The island beckons all seeking the ultimate romantic escape!

Let Bali Wedding Planners make your Dream Wedding come true.

Imagine making your wedding vows in one of our exclusive private villas overlooking the Indian Ocean, after a ride on a majestic elephant or during an exotic Royal Balinese ceremony. We can handle everything from start to finish as we help to arrange your most important day as a couple. Over 10 years of experience.

The One-Stop Wedding Boutique
Our modern wedding store is dedicated to serving the discerning bride and groom. From dresses and suits to legal formalities, catering, entertainment, decorations, make-up, hair styling, flowers, photo and video shoots, we will plan all this for you in great detail.

For a perfect finale, indulge in a totally romantic honeymoon getaway on one of the many nearby islands, or at an idyllic mountain retreat.

Legal Requirements for A Wedding in Indonesia

All couples who marry in Indonesia must declare a religion. Agnosticism and Atheism are not recognized. The Civil Registry Office can record marriages of persons of Islam, Hindu, Buddhist, Christian-Protestant and Christian-Catholic faiths. Marriage partners must have the same religion; otherwise one partner must make a written declaration of a change of religion.

The Religious Marriage under Islam is performed by the Office of Religious Affairs (Kantor Urusan Agama) in a ceremony at a mosque, the home, a restaurant, or any other place chosen by the couple and is legal immediately after the ceremony.

A Christian, Hindu or Buddhist marriage is usually performed first in a church or temple ceremony. After the religious ceremony, every non-Islamic marriage must be recorded with the Civil Registry (Kantor Catatan Sipil). Without the registration by the Civil Registry these marriages are not legal. Recording by Civil Registry officials can be performed directly at the religious ceremony for an additional fee.

Persons of non-Islamic faith are required to file with the Civil Registry Office in the Regency where they are staying, first a 'Notice of Intention to Marry' as well as a 'Letter of No Impediment' obtained from their consular representatives.

For the issue of the Letter of No Impediment to Marriage by your Consular Representative you will need to present for yourself and your fiancé(e) your Passport(s) valid for more than 6 months and Certified Divorce Decrees (absolute/final) and/or Death Certificates regarding the termination of any previous marriages. Please contact the Consular Representative of your country for details well before the intended date of marriage.

Indonesia Information

For the Notice of Intention to Marry you have to submit the following documents for both partners to the Civil Registry Office (show the original and present a photocopy):

- Certificate of the religious marriage;
- Passport for foreign citizens, or KTP (Identity card) for Indonesian citizens;
- Certified birth certificate;
- Certified divorce decree (absolute) or death certificates regarding the termination of all previous marriages;
- Four 4x6 cm photos, both partners side by side;
- Foreign citizens:
- Letter of No Impediment to Marriage issued by your Consular Representative for Bali or Indonesia;
- Indonesian citizens:
- Never married: letter Surat Keterangan Belum Kawin from Kepala Desa or Lurah (mayor);

> Men aged 18-21 and women aged 16-21: parental letter of consent, signed across the meterai/tax stamp Rupiah 2,000.

Before the marriage, you and your fiancé(e) may also wish to file, with the Civil Registry, a prenuptial Property Agreement (Surat Pernyataan Harta) which must be signed before a local Notary Public. This contract is necessary if you wish to hold property separately during the marriage. In the absence of such a document, Indonesian marriage law assumes joint ownership of property, and subsequent property acquisitions by the Indonesian partner will be regulated according to the laws restricting foreign property ownership.

Two witnesses over the age of 18 are required. They must show the originals and present photocopies of their passports if they are foreign citizens or KTP (identity cards) if they are Indonesian citizens. Civil Registry employees can also act as witnesses.

The Civil Registry office has a Mandatory Waiting Period of 10 working days from the date of filing. This waiting period may be waived for tourists presenting a guest registration form (Form A).

Islamic Marriage Certificates (Buku Nikah) issued by the Office of Religious Affairs (Kantor Urusan Agama) are legally valid in Indonesia and do not require registration with any other agency if you are going to live in Indonesia. However, if you might move somewhere else in the future (and who knows?), get a marriage certificate issued by the Civil Registry and an officially certified translation right away (see below).

All other Marriage Certificates will be issued by the Civil Registry usually on the same or next day. A sworn English translation of the marriage certificate should be obtained for use abroad. It is not necessary for the marriage certificate or translation to be registered by your Consular Agency. However, to have the sworn translation of the marriage certificate verified or a special translation made by the Consular Agency of your home country, or the Consular Agency of your country of residence, might prove useful.

Weddings at The St Regis Bali Resort - Bali

Cloud Nine Chapel

Celebrate the most memorable day in your life at the *Cloud Nine Chapel,* a wedding chapel set directly overlooking the pristine and exclusive beachfront at St. Regis Bali. The Swarovski crystal chandeliers hanging from the high ceiling and the magnificent views of the ocean from the Cloud Nine Chapel create a magical and unmatched atmosphere that is sophisticated and at the same time intimate.

Designed to accentuate the beauty of the setting, the *Cloud Nine Chapel* is surrounded by a tranquil pond fed by four water fountains, with overflowing water that soothingly cascades down each step, exuding a calm feeling that is relaxing on the eye.

A stylish timber terrace, the *Cloud Nine Terrace* lies beyond the pond, right at the beachfront, providing guests with an ideal venue to have pre-dinner canapés and a refreshing beverage, or simply a champagne wedding toast.

Amphitheatre
The *Amphitheatre* is surrounded by lush tropical gardens, offering a perfect setting for a magical garden wedding ceremony with an elegant white and green theme. The wedding venue is designed for a large group of up to 80 guests celebrating in theatre style. Complement your event with soft background music entertainment until 7:00pm.

Details

Barefoot on the Beach
Imagine your enchanting beachfront wedding on soft white sands, set against azure waters and complemented by a gentle sea breeze that truly epitomises sultry island romance. Within this dazzling, yet very private world of romantic splendour, your

senses are enhanced by captivating flower decorations, featuring tropical Balinese frangipani flowers or elegant roses in delicate shades of ivory, leaving you with a memorable and cherished dream.

Details

More Wedding Options and Packages
Music and Entertainment - Wedding Staff can arrange
Trio Jazz Band (Guitar, Keyboard, and Saxophone)
DJ (Jazz and Chilled Music)
Trio Classic (Violin, Guitar, Saxophone)
Legong Dance
Rindik Gamelan
Photographer and videographer can also be arranged.

RUDYLIN Photography & Video Motion - Bali

Rudy Lin is the founder of Rudy Lin Photography. He is a graduate of Graphic Design College and a person who loves playing with camera, light and special moments. A Bali-Jakarta based photographer who welcomes overseas photo sessions, Rudy Lin has a huge passion for telling the artistic story behind the lens. Youth, spirit and hard work become one vision to be proven in each photo with clean, minimalist modern and elegant style.

He regards each photo as a lovely way to capture a new story, more than as a witness or invitee. His style and attention to detail and atmosphere makes each photo a long lasting and timeless memory.

RUDYLIN is a trademark for professional wedding photography, especially in Bali. Rudylin offers professional services in Photography, Videography, Wedding Organization, Bridal Boutique, Makeup and Hair Styling, as well as other wedding services.

RUDYLIN styles are more candid and natural, with attention to details and the atmosphere of your wedding day. We would love to present unbelievable moments for you, because we believe each couple is different and unique. That is why all our pictures will represent you as the happiest bride and groom ever!

PRICING:

We offer 3 hour, 6 hour, 9 hour and 12 hour packages, plus video. On average we usually provide 400-500 images for a full-day wedding. All wedding packages include a second photographer or lighting assistant, who assists photographer to get other angles or even multiple moments.

All of our photo and video packages include a DVD with high-resolution digital files (original & edited photos) and we have a number of packages available: Wedding Photo Package or Prewedding Photo Package, plus Videomotion Package for your big day.

Associate Make-Up Artist and Wedding Organizer in Bali.

We have exclusive contracts with makeup artist, bridal and other vendors in Bali. Makeup artist - Cindy Lin Makeup & Beauty. Wedding Organizer - Bali Passion Wedding & Events. Bridal and Gown rental - Lines Bridal Boutique

White Door Wedding Gallery - Bali

White Door is the leading wedding dress boutique chain from Japan, stocking imported wedding dresses. With shops in major cities all over Japan, and in Rome, and Florence, White Door has the edge in the wedding market. Now also at the Ritz-Carlton Resort & Spa in Jimbaran, Bali.

WEDDING GALLERY

Studio 5 - Wedding Dress White Door imports wedding dresses from the ateliers of nine of the world's leading wedding designers in Paris, Rome, New York and Tokyo, and these are always in stock in Bali's largest and most luxurious wedding boutique. Choose from a selection of hundreds of world-class wedding dresses for your big day. Studio 5 also stocks a large collection of evening gowns and tuxedos, plus a range of imported formal wear and accessories.

White Door is also one of the world's leading wedding organizers, organizing weddings in 25 world capitals in

Asia, Europe, Australia, and the Americas, so they can organize every aspect of your wedding, from photography and videography using their in-house team of professionals, to flower decorations by Massa Flowers, cake, paper items, menu co-ordination — trying always to work within your budget.

Photo Studio

White Door Photo Studio is the first world-class photo studio in Bali, offering full digital photo capabilities and in-house printing capabilities using the latest equipment from Japan. The large team of in-house videographers and photographers working within White Door have been trained by professionals from Japan and are considered the best in Indonesia.

All the pre-wedding and wedding services:

Pre-Wedding, Full legal wedding, Civil wedding, Religious wedding, Commitment ceremony, Renewal of vows

OPTIONAL SERVICES:

Dress and tuxedo, Hair and make-up artist, Professional wedding photographer and videographer, Floral artist, Wedding cakes, Catering.

Weddings at Ubud Hanging Gardens - Bali

Ubud Hanging Gardens provides exceptional surroundings for an unforgettable event. Experience the perfect setting for your Balinese wedding and for a truly romantic honeymoon. Let our Wedding Team create a unique floating wedding, set on our horizon-edge pool, or magical moments on the terrace with dramatic views over the Ayung River valley.

Whether you select a traditional wedding or an intimate ceremony, Ubud Hanging Gardens can provide an expert coordinator and full catering services to make wedding planning effortless. Include our pre-wedding spa package and turn your special day into a delightful experience.

WEDDING PACKAGES

LEGAL WEDDING PACKAGE

Includes: Wedding assistant, venue, decorations, corsage, bouquet, and legal arrangements (religious minister certificate, civil certificate and document processing)

Price: from US$2,750. Service charges, tax and gratuities are not included.

COMMITMENT CEREMONY PACKAGE

Includes: Wedding assistant, venue, decoration, corsage and bouquet

Price: from US$1,900. Service charges, tax and gratuities are not included.

TYPE OF WEDDING:

- International legal wedding
- Balinese legal wedding
- Commitment ceremony

DECORATION:

- Balinese decoration - local flowers and leaves, coconut leaves and other local products
- Western decoration – Western-style flower theme
- VENUE:
- Floating wedding - set above the Infinity Pool on a floating stage
- Enchanted temple wedding - set in the Balinese temple across the river from the resort
- Enchanted Valley wedding – set in the Diatas Pohon Café
- Private in-villa wedding - located on your villa's pool deck

HONEYMOONS

Ubud Hanging Gardens is the ultimate tropical destination for the most romantic honeymoon you could imagine. Experience the beauty and tranquillity of the jungle, toast the new day with a champagne breakfast in bed, indulge in a Secret Romantic Dinner, awaken the senses with our Romantic Hideaway spa package. The possibilities are endless. With luxurious and intimate villas, each with its own private heated infinity pool, Ubud Hanging Gardens is the ultimate tropical destination for the ideal honeymoon.

HONEYMOON PACKAGE

Includes: Luxury accommodation; One-way airport transfer; Speedy visa assistance; Flower petal welcome; Gift upon arrival; Balinese welcome drink; Daily buffet breakfast for two; One romantic 3-course dinner in the Beduur restaurant; One private picnic; One traditional Balinese couples massage; Use of mountain bikes and shuttle to Ubud centre (on schedule); Fresh tropical fruit in your room. Two-night minimum stay required

The three treatment pavilions at AYUNG SPA are surrounded by verdant gardens and have been designed using local materials. Surrender to the secrets of Balinese well-being at Ayung Spa, where state-of-the-art facilities and the balancing powers of nature deliver a truly luxurious experience for the two of you.

For ADVENTUROUS COUPLES we also offer an Early Morning Botanical Walk, Rural Bali Experience, Ayung River Rafting, Batur Volcano Ascent, Bali Bird Park visit, Golf at Handara Kosaido, Touring and Shopping in Ubud, Yoga, Painting classes and Cookery classes.

Wangi Bali Wedding Organizer and Co. - Bali

Wangi Bali Wedding Organizer and Co. is a fully equipped wedding company with divisions covering all aspects of the Wedding Industry. Wangi Bali was established primarily to assist foreigners who choose to marry in Bali. The company's experienced professionals offer the highest level of service right across the beautiful Island of Bali. Wangi Bali offers the best wedding locations for our clients, whether for a Chapel Wedding, Hotel Wedding or Villa Wedding. Our sole raison d'étre is to satisfy our customers by catering to all their needs so that their wedding celebration will be the most memorable time of their lives.

OUR SERVICES

1. Bridal make up and salon. 2. Our own Gown collection (50 to 100 gowns). 3. Designers to make custom gowns. 4. Professional photographers, pre-wedding photography, photo studio, photo documentation, fashion photography, and concept photography. 5. Video with documentation. 6. Nail art decoration, nail painting, design sculpture 3D, nail extension, aquarium extensions. 7. Legal wedding documentation. 8. Entertainment, MC, sound systems, dancers (Balinese dancing, modern dancing), live music (Jazz, classic, local, etc.). 9. Wedding decorations. 10. Catering (food, beverage) 11. Wedding cakes. 12. Invitation cards. 13. Transportation (limo, etc.) 14. Memorable souvenirs. 15. Balinese traditional weddings.

HOTEL WEDDINGS

We organise weddings at these hotels:

Le Meridien Nirwana at Tanah Lot, Mèlia Benoa, Novotel Benoa, Samaya at Seminyak, Santika Premiere Beach Resort, Sanur Beach Hotel, The Legian at Seminyak, Oasis at Tanjung Benoa.

CHAPEL WEDDINGS

Bluemoon Wedding Chapel at Oceanblue Hotel, The Diamond Wedding Pavilion located in Sanur Area, Blue Point Chapel, Infinity Chapel at the Conrad Bali, the Mirage Chapel at Mirage Resort & Thalasso Bali, The Vimala Wedding Pavilion at Ubud Village, Wiwaha Wedding Chapel at Nikko Bali Resort & Spa.

VILLA WEDDINGS

GAJAH PUTIH - Villa Gajah Putih is one of Bali's most prestigious properties. This 6-bedroom estate is set on over an acre and half of beachfront land, with a tennis court, home cinema and 20 staff.

INDAH MANIS - Together, Indah Manis and Bulan Madu provide a luxurious 6 bedroom retreat in southern Bali, providing the comforts of a private home and the service standards of a fine boutique hotel.

ISTANA VILLA - is located on the south-western tip of Bali, in an area called The Bukit Peninsula. This 5 suite estate overlooks white sand beaches and a lagoon abundant with sea life and coral, and in the evenings, magical sunsets.

KHAYANGAN VILLA - is on a cliff-top against the spectacular backdrop of the Indian Ocean with beautiful sunsets. The perfect place for your wedding ceremony.

PUSPA PURI VILLA - On the beachfront, near the traditional village of Ketewel, Sanur, just 45 minutes drive from Bali's International airport, 30 minutes from the cultural town of Ubud.

UMAH DE BIJI - is a magnificent, tranquil property of exceptional visual appeal. The size and design of the grounds provides for many secluded seating areas making this villa the perfect location for large groups of friends or family.

VILLA ATAS OMBAK - Indonesian for 'Villa on The Waves,' provides seaside luxury with breathtaking views of Bali's famous sunsets. One of the most outstanding luxury villas on Bali.

VILLA HANANI - romantic and secluded venue with panoramic view of white sand beach, blue ocean and magnificent sunset. The perfect place to celebrate your memorable day.

ADDITIONAL SERVICES

Catering, Entertainment – Balinese music, Balinese dancers or modern music, Flower girls, Hair and make-up, Wedding dresses, Wedding decorations, Wedding cake, pre-wedding Spa treatment, Photography and videography, Wedding gift arrangements.

CEREMONIES ARRANGED

Religious wedding for all faiths, Civil wedding, Commitment ceremony, Full legal wedding, Renewal of Vows

SUNSET WEDDINGS at Kuta, Legian, Seminyak

Weddings at Ayana Resort and Spa Bali - Bali

Welcome to one of the top luxury hotels in Bali. Some reasons why you should celebrate your wedding here.

CONDE NAST TRAVELLER READERS' AWARDS

2011 Best Resort in Asia.

2010 #1 Spa Resort in the World.

WORLD TRAVEL AWARDS 2011.

Indonesia's Leading Resort & Indonesia's Leading Spa Resort.

2010 Asia's Leading Luxury Resort & Asia's Leading Luxury Villa (AYANA Villa).

TRAVEL + LEISURE 2010 World's Top 20 Hotels for Overall Value.

THE YAK READERS' AWARDS 2011 Best Sunset Venue - Rock Bar Bali.

ASEAN - ASSOCIATION OF SOUTH-EAST ASIAN NATIONS 2010 ASEAN Green Hotel Recognition Award

Hidden in 77 hectares of cliff-top tropical gardens 35 meters above Jimbaran Bay, AYANA Resort and Spa Bali enjoys majestic views from a secluded location, boasting 209 resort rooms, 10 resort suites, 71 club rooms and suites, and 78 villas. Each room at our Bali luxury resort harmoniously blends the latest modern comforts with traditional design, which is highlighted in Indonesian carving, sculpture, paintings and artefacts.

Every room has a private balcony. The marbled bathroom contains separate rain shower and deep soaking bathtub. Bedding is either King-sized or twin double beds. Amenities include 42-inch flat-screen television, writing table, aromatic burner set and mini-bar.

For a completely indulgent romantic wedding and honeymoon, escape to the best resort in Bali, dine at lavish restaurants, enjoy boundless recreation, or just relax in our five-star hotel in Bali with no schedule except your next treatment at the 'Thermes Marins Spa' and award-winning 'Spa on the Rocks'. Enjoy our 6 swimming pools and 12 restaurants..

Enchanting Bali Hotel WEDDING PACKAGES - Unforgettable Events

Top of the list of the World's Best Wedding Venues by CNNGo, AYANA Resort and Spa Bali is renowned for its shimmering glass chapels, elite wedding planners, Rock Bar after-parties, and awesome views. Rates amongst the world's most enchanting wedding venues for its ability to offer truly unique and memorable celebrations, unmatched anywhere else in the world. From intimate family celebrations to grand ballroom galas, our oceanfront venues set a captivating stage for unforgettable Bali weddings . A choice of 7 different venues, including 2 glass chapels, stunning presidential private wedding villa, 350-year-old Javanese 'joglo', traditional Balinese Pavilion, the vibrant Champa Garden, or our Private Jetty for an intimate ceremony just for two. Let our professional wedding planners organise your special day and produce a memorable start to your life together.

STORYBOOK WEDDING OPTIONS

AYANA Resort and Spa sets a truly enchanting stage for Bali hotel weddings, including a horse-drawn 'Cindarella Carriage' to 'take you away' after your fairytale wedding.. AYANA Resort also offers a Wedding Gift Registry service, where wedding guests can contribute to a honeymoon package you will cherish forever.

'SOMETHING NEW' Ayana Villa Wedding

People are often searching for gifts to satisfy the tradition of having 'Something old, something new, something borrowed, something blue' for luck on their wedding day, so unique experiences are at the heart of the 'Something New' Bali Wedding Package at AYANA Villa, the 3-bedroom presidential villa set on 3000sqm of cliff-top land over Jimbaran Bay. With this honeymoon wedding package, couples will share special moments not only on their wedding day, but also before and after it, such as creating their own signature fragrance at AYANA's perfume-making studio, and escaping to Rock Bar Bali for sunset cocktails.

Enjoy accommodation at the breathtaking AYANA Villa for your ceremony, reception and honeymoon, all in one private, secure location. Exclusive services for AYANA Villa guests include open bar with top shelf liquors, chefs for private dinner parties, spa treatment room, fitness room, and 24-hour dedicated butler service accredited by the Guild of Professional Butlers in the UK (think royalty and celebrity-style service).

SWEET ESCAPE WEDDING

Enjoy an intimate ceremony for two Robinson Crusoe 'castaways' at the end of AYANA's private jetty. For those wanting to celebrate in a more intimate setting, this venue makes for an extremely romantic and personal exchange of vows as you embark on your new life together.

KISIK JETTY is the only private pier in Bali available for hotel wedding ceremonies. Entry to this magical location starts with a descent to sea level via AYANA's inclinator, which provides sensational views across the coastline as it descends the cliff-face to the beach below. A path leads to a wooden jetty stretching 30 metres out to sea, decorated with your preferred floral arrangements. At the end of the pier, Balinese penjor (ceremonial poles) rise up into the sky, as soft music from bamboo xylophones accompanies the sound of the ocean waves gently rolling towards the beach underneath you. Imagine jetting off from here in a 'James Bond' boat.

SECRET GARDEN WEDDING

Choose a romantic and private 'Secret Garden' hotel wedding in Bali to declare your cherished promises of love. Lush exotic fragrant flowers and an endless stretch of sparkling Indian Ocean surround sunset glows and provide a magical setting for fabulous Bali destination weddings.

ASMARA - This outdoor venue is distinguished by its decorative 350 year old 'joglo' - a ceremonial pavilion - a feature of the Royal Palaces of central Java.

BALÉ KENCANA - With 180-degree views of the Indian Ocean, this traditional Bali wedding site is surrounded by tropical gardens hidden behind stone walls. Surrounded by a tranquil pond and natural stone paving, the raised thatch-roofed gazebo provides an open-air stage for the bridal couple, with theatre-style seating for guests in front.

SUNSET PROMISE WEDDING - Feel like Cinderella and Prince Charming as you make your vows in one of our 2 glass panelled Wedding Pavilions backed by an Indian Ocean horizon. From the towering cliffs of Jimbaran Bay, shimmering sunsets and stunning vistas offer picture perfect backdrops to these stylish locations

TRESNA WEDDING CHAPEL - is a dramatically-illuminated chapel that towers above the Indian Ocean. Its see-through glass centre-aisle with stone-lined river underneath leads to a magnificent glass altar. Fully air-conditioned, with seating for up to 50 people inside.

ASTINA WEDDING CHAPEL - Surrounded by water features and amazing Indian Ocean views, the glass-sided, indoor Astina wedding chapel is in striking Asian Modern design. Fully air-conditioned with adjacent

Bridal Villa, private driveway and porte-cochere, seats up to 80 people.

CHAMPA GARDEN is an avant-garde 20,000sqm outdoor area designed to host grand scale wedding ceremonies and receptions. With a capacity to cater 3,000-plus guests in complete seclusion, this grand Bali hotel wedding venue is the first and largest private outdoor venue of its kind created within the grounds of a five-star hotel, built with 2,000 white frangipani trees surrounding it. A paved avenue leads past tranquil water features to a grand stage overlooking the expansive gardens. Most suitable for a Bolliwood-style wedding, with Balinese music and dancers in colourful costumes if you so wish.

The End

www.ingramcontent.com/pod-product-compliance
Lightning Source LLC
Chambersburg PA
CBHW031059080526
44587CB00011B/747